NEW FOODS
for
HEALTHY EATING

NEW FOODS
for
HEALTHY EATING

A Consumer's Guide

Liz Brand

BISHOPSGATE PRESS LIMITED

DEDICATION

To my family
– for their ever enduring support

Cover photographs by kind permission of C.O.L.E.A.C.P.

Line illustrations and design by G & G Graphics.

© 1987 Liz Brand

Brand, Elizabeth
    New foods for healthy eating.
    1. Food, Natural – Great Britain
    I. Title
    641.3'02'0941   TX369

    ISBN 1-85219-010-8

All enquiries and requests relevant to this title should be sent to the publisher, Bishopsgate Press Ltd., 37 Union Street, London SE1 1SE

Printed by Whitstable Litho Ltd., Whitstable, Kent.

Contents

Introduction

A quick glance around today's supermarket shelves reveals a bewildering range, not just of revamped old favourites but genuine new ingredients which have been introduced slowly via specialist and health food stores. The combination of improved transportation, packaging and storage techniques have played their part in ensuring this, as has the crescendo in numbers of multiracial inhabitants who have brought with them a demand for the flavours of their far off homelands. Added to this, the recent opportunities for more widespread travel has softened the once general antipathy towards experimenting with unfamiliar foods.

Information on many of these ingredients, covering grains, dairy products, beverages, sweeteners, the ever increasing wealth of fruits and vegetables, seeds, nuts and pulses is somewhat scarce, as are practical suggestions for their implementation into today's eating patterns. The following pages offer a guide as to how best to choose and prepare these ingredients, along with recipe ideas suitable for a range of occasions, interesting background information concerning their history and any processing techniques involved before the products reach the shop shelves. By providing the knowledge necessary for a comprehensive understanding of these commodities it is hoped that full advantage will subsequently be taken of their benefits.

Inextricably tied to the use of each ingredient and their value in cookery is the nutritional contribution which they make to the diet. Since, where practical, the primary nutrients of each food have been included, outlined below is a brief resumé of their basic functions:

Protein – necessary for growth and repair of the body's tissues, excess protein is converted into energy. It also provides a back up source of energy should there be an insufficient intake of carbohydrates.

Carbohydrates – a source of energy, they include sugars, starch and fibrous materials.

Fibre – worthy of a special mention since, although of no nutritional value as it is indigestible, fibre plays an important role in hastening the transit time of digested food matter through the intestinal tract. As a general guide refined foods will have had the majority of their natural fibre removed. There are many different forms of fibre including cellulose, lignin (predominant in root vegetables) and pectin (found in fruit).

Fats – a more concentrated form of energy than carbohydrates they contain the fat soluble vitamins A, D, E and K.

Minerals – although present only in minute amounts minerals are essential for health and vitality. The most important include:
Calcium which is necessary for the formation of strong bones and teeth.
Iron, a deficiency of which results in anaemia – manifesting itself in tiredness and giddy spells – since iron is necessary for the formation of red blood cells, which in turn carry oxygen around the body.

Vitamins – again only small quantities are required and deficiencies are rare in this country. However, because the water soluble vitamins cannot be stored in the body daily intakes are necessary.
Vitamin A is chemically known as retinol. Carotene, found in fruit, vegetables and milk is converted to retinol in the body. Vitamin A plays a vital part in good vision and skin complexion.
B group vitamins are involved in the release and utilisation of energy derived from food. They ensure efficient functioning of the nervous and circulatory system and the brain and contribute towards general good health – bright hair and eyes.
Vitamin B12 plays an important role in the formation of blood. Since this nutrient is not present in vegetable foods vegans vegetarians may need a vitamin tablet supplement.
Vitamin C is essential for the formation of the body's connective tissue as well as for healthy gums and skin. Its presence facilitates the absorption of iron.
Vitamin D is vital for the body's absorption of calcium and phosphorus and therefore has an indirect effect on bones and teeth.
Vitamin E plays a part in the body's all round basic metabolism in particular protecting the tissues and blood.
Vitamin K is necessary for clotting of the blood.

Although by no means a wholefood book, it has been written following the dietary advice of the time. Traditional favourites – such as pastries and cakes, which tend to be high in fat and sugar – have been included but in a modified form, by reducing the levels of these high calorific ingredients whilst increasing the amount of fibre. By using natural yoghurt as a replacement or extender for cream, a reduction in fat, as well as cost, is achieved. Where possible use fruit instead of sugar to sweeten, fats which are high in polyunsaturates rather than saturated animal fats and unprocessed grains such as wholemeal flour and brown rice. Through introduction of these simple substitutes the essence of familiar dishes can be maintained without losing sight of the importance of their palatability.

The diversity of the number of potential new foods – whether they be imported from around the world, or a process of modern technology – makes the enormity of this book's task daunting. Even more so because not all of those ingredients introduced will stay, their survival depending on economic as well as practical suitability to today's style of cookery. However, the majority of ingredients, which will find a place in the kitchen, offer an exciting basis for dishes with a new look. By combining them with the more established foods their cost (particularly as is the case for many fruits and vegetables) can be reduced, and original recipes created for use in everyday cooking.

CHAPTER 1

——Cereals and Grasses——

As an inexpensive and versatile form of energy, cereals provide the basis of diets throughout the world. The varieties grown in a particular country depend on the climate, although, in most cases better farming techniques, coupled with the cultivation of more than one cereal, has ensured that famines are mainly history.

The word cereals stems from the Goddess Ceres, giver of the earth's bounties, who was worshipped by the Romans. At one time staple grains were peculiar to certain countries – for example, rye was scarcely eaten outside Scandinavia and Germany. Then the conquerors, explorers and settlers travelled with the grasses which they had cultivated, effectively introducing alternative strains which are now taken for granted. In the case of wheat, it is interesting that originally it was only the nobility who could afford to eat white bread, from which the bran and wheatgerm had been removed, and the poor had to make do with brown. Whereas nowadays white bread is less expensive and consumed in greater quantities, although sales of wholemeal and brown are increasing.

Basically a carbohydrate food (70-80%), cereals provide energy. They are also rich in the B group of vitamins, protein and minerals, in particular calcium and iron. Flours from whole grains are a valuable source of natural fibre. Being low in fat, on average cereals contain 1-2%, their nutritional composition is very favourable when considering the current dietary guidelines to eat more fibre while decreasing the consumption of fat, sugar and salt.

Cereals are versatile in that they can be milled in a variety of ways to produce several different products, such as flakes, meal, flour or groats.

Generally speaking, whole grains keep longer than when milled into flour. Both grains and flour should be stored in a cool, dark, dry place, preferably in airtight containers.

BARLEY

Once the dominant bread grain of the Ancient Greeks and Romans, wheat and rye flour gradually replaced barley until by the Middle Ages its contribution to the diet was minimal. Only a few areas, such as the Scottish Highlands, now farm a sizeable area. The crop grows well on poor, well drained soil, with the grains use being mainly confined to soups and stews. France, Australia and Canada are the largest exporters, while abroad barley is a valuable food in Asia, the Middle and Far East and North Africa. The small barley grain is white in colour with a beige crevice down its length. Pearl barley, groats, flakes and flour are produced from milling: after cleaning the grain is conditioned and shelled, to remove the outer layer of husk, producing pot barley. Pearling, when the remaining husk and some of the endosperm is scoured away, gives the shiny pearl barley which has to be polished between sandstones. Barley flakes are produced by steaming pearl barley and flattening it between smooth rollers. Pot barley therefore has a higher nutritional content than pearl (the majority of protein, calcium, iron and B vitamins being in the aleurone layer which remains intact), and takes longer to cook. Barley flour and groats are also available. Barley has a fine texture and is slightly sweet. Being particularly easy to digest it is consequently recommended for baby and invalid foods. It is popular in soups and hot pots whereas flaked barley gives a pleasant flavour to hot milk puddings. However, the major uses of barley are for animal feed, beer making and whisky distillation. Malt extract is a product of the first stage of beer making where the barley is malted. Barley water, which can be flavoured with fruit juices, is made by simmering 2oz (50g) pot barley in 1 pint (600ml) water until the liquid is reduced by half.

BUCKWHEAT

Primarily cultivated in Asia from whence it was brought to Europe in the Middle Ages by the crusaders, hence its alternative name – Saracen Corn, buckwheat is a type of grass, not a true cereal, but for culinary purposes is classified as one. Related to sorrel, rhubarb and dock, buckwheat grows well on poor soil in Russia, Africa and Germany. The seeds resemble tiny beechnuts, triangular in shape and beige-silver in colour, they are sold as groats or flour and have a distinctive taste. The harvested seeds are washed, dried and their husks removed to give groats, before being milled into flour. The groats may be sold toasted, when they are known by their Russian name of "kasha", or raw. Their main use is for a type of porridge although they are ideal for stuffing vegetables; roasted in a little oil until nutty and simmered in 4 parts stock to 1 part buckwheat for 20-25 minutes with onion, carrot and

French beans, or served in place of rice. Buckwheat flour is the basic ingredient of another Russian favourite, "blinis" (savoury pancakes), and may be used in muffins and biscuits. It does not contain gluten and thus gives a heavy textured result, so is often combined with wheat flour. Due to the difficulty of separating the husk the flour is grey-purple in colour and more expensive than most other cereal flours. Buckwheat spaghetti, "soba", which is popular in Japan, can be used instead of durum wheat for pasta, but requires a longer cooking time. The presence of rutic acid in buckwheat has a beneficial effect on the arteries and circulatory system. The grain is fairly high in protein, iron and the B group of vitamins.

LEMON GRASS

An aromatic grass, native to South East Asia, main imports come from Thailand. Lemon grass consists of many broad, tightly wrapped blades of lemon scented leaves with a diameter of about ½" (12.5mm) at the base. To prepare; peel off dryish outside blades, trim to a length of 6" (15cm), and bruise with a knife to release citrus oils. Lemon grass is usually sold in bunches and may be used to flavour fish dishes, curries, soups and sauces, rubbed around the inside of a salad bowl, infused in boiling water to make lemon tea, or added to milk puddings. The grass is usually removed before serving but can be finely chopped and incorporated into the dish. Wrap closely, since it's flavour tends to pervade other ingredients and store in a cool place for up to two weeks.

MAIZE

For centuries the staple of the Aztecs, Incas and Maya's diet, maize is now an important African food. It grows well in Europe and America and is also cultivated in India, Africa and Australia. After wheat and rice, maize is the world's largest crop, America being the main producer. Once the cereal has been cleaned and conditioned the oil is extracted from the grain's germ, thus prolonging its shelf life. This oil forms a valuable by product (corn oil). The grain is then milled, as for wheat, to produce maize flour, which contains about 7% protein. Maize meal (also known as corn meal) is the hulled grain, coarsely ground and sieved, and is yellow in colour because the germ has not been removed, consequently it does tend towards rancidity. It has a granular texture, somewhat similar to semolina and its nutritional value is higher than wheat. Maize meal forms the basic ingredient of polenta – a gruel much favoured in Italy, where it combines with water and salt and is simmered for 20-30 minutes. Sweet or savoury ingredients may be added. When cold the polenta is traditionally cut into squares and fried. In Mexico maize meal is used to make tortillas, a type of pancake. Normally the niacin present is unavailable to the body, but the conventional method adopted, of steeping the flour in lime, ensures that it is released and the risk of pellagra to the natives avoided. Maize meal is free from gluten and makes golden coloured biscuits, muffins and cakes when mixed with wheat flour.

MILLET

Often looked upon as bird feed in this country, millet was in fact originally the staple food of China before rice. One of the earliest cereals used for human consumption it still remains a vital food in Africa, Asia and Central America. Once the grain has been harvested the very hard outer casing is removed since it is inedible and contains no valuable nutrients. The grain is then either left whole in the form of tiny pellets; flaked, by crushing between rollers; or milled into flour. Since millet has a fairly high fat content it will not keep for long, especially in the form of flakes. Wash and drain the millet before cooking in plenty of boiling water as for rice, until the grains are white and fluffy, 15-25 minutes. Millet readily absorbs water which means that a little goes a long way. Its flavour can be enhanced by roasting the washed millet to dry it, and then frying in a little oil before adding the water. Nutritionally millet contains a fair amount of iron and is also a source of protein, calcium and B vitamins. It contributes a little fibre to the diet. The grains may be substituted for rice, and the flakes added to cakes and muesli. Millet flour is a good thickening agent, also adding a rich colour to soups and casseroles. Since millet is low in gluten it must be mixed with wheat flour for breadmaking.

OATS

Although still held in high esteem in Scotland, oats no longer enjoy as widespread usage as in the past. To produce oats for human consumption the hairy beard which covers the grain is first removed. Then, because of the relatively high fat content of oats compared with other cereals, the grain is steamed and dried, thus prolonging its shelf life, before being husked. Whole grains, groats, flakes and meal are available. Oats cannot be milled in the same manner as wheat, whose chaff is easily removed during threshing, because their fibrous husk is inedible. Oatmeal is made by cleaning the grain and then stabilising it by deactivating the enzymes which cause deterioration. It is then dried in a kiln to give an authentic flavour before being polished and shelled – a process in which the grains are crushed, splitting the husk from the groat. The kernel/groat is split into 4–5 pieces known as pinhead meal. Medium and fine oatmeal are the products of further grinding. Oats have a low extraction rate, about 55%, because of the necessary removal of the husk. However, they are high in protein, fat, iron, calcium and B group vitamins. Oat flakes/rolled oats are made from pinhead oatmeal which is cooked in a steamer to soften the particles, before being flattened between hot rollers. This shortens their cooking time. Oatmeal bran is pale and less coarse than wheat bran. When cooked the grain has a slimy texture and is easily digestible. It is also known to have a beneficial effect on the digestive system. Oats are free from gluten. Oat flakes are delicious in cold or hot muesli while oatmeal combines well with wheat flour to give a nutty pastry, can be used as a coating for food or as part of a nut loaf mixture.

RICE

Cultivated in ancient India, Japan and China, where it is recorded to have been grown as long ago as 2800 BC, rice vies with wheat as the world's most widely used cereal. Yet it was only 300 years ago that explorers introduced it into this country, chiefly as an accompaniment to the hot spicy foods which they brought back with them from their travels. Rice flourishes in a hot, wet climate and hence grows well in tropical regions, Canada and the USA. Indeed America is the largest exporter. Many varieties of rice exist and are usually grown on swamp land, although some strains do well on dry land. The seeds of the harvested grass are dried and cleaned before the husk and bran are removed by abrasive scouring of the outer layer to produce unpolished rice, known as brown rice, which is silver/fawn in colour. This leaves the second husk where the fibre, fat, protein, B vitamins and minerals are stored. White rice, which has been polished, has had the second husk removed leaving a shiny grain which consists mainly of starch and is consequently easily digested. Brown rice will not keep for as long as white because its higher fat content encourages rancidity. Flakes and rice flour are obtained by further milling of the polished rice and are suitable for milk puddings and porridge type dishes. Rice flour adds a crunchy bite to biscuits – substitute for a little wheat flour. Brown rice flour, made with the whole grain, is also available. Basmati rice, a white, long, narrow grain provides an ideal accompaniment to savoury dishes instead of potatoes or pasta. It is best soaked for ½ hour before simmering in boiling water for about 20 minutes. Brown rice takes 45-50 minutes to cook* and is excellent in risotto. Wild rice, usually sold blended with long grain white rice because of its expense, due to shortage of supply, is the seed of an aquatic grass grown in muddy swamps, and in streams and lakes in North America. It is purple-black in colour and has a strong flavour. Rice is roughly categorised into short or long grain. The former, also known as round rice, being suitable for puddings, because of its slightly sticky, soft texture when cooked, and long grain, Patna rice for savoury dishes – risotto, paella, pilau or as a stuffing. In order to preserve as many nutrients as possible it is best to cook rice in only as much water/stock as it can absorb, therefore as a guide use 1 part rice to 3 parts water. The rice should be rinsed before cooking to remove any loose starch which causes the cooked grains to stick together. 2oz (50g) uncooked rice per person is sufficient.

*(although quick cooking types which take only 20 minutes are now available)

RYE

It was the Romans who cultivated the rye which they found growing like a weed when they invaded Britain. During the Middle Ages ergot fungus infected the grain, causing widespread plagues. The common form of bread at this time consisted of blended rye and barley and was known as maslin. The cereal grows on infertile soil and flourishes in Siberia and Northern Europe, Germany and Canada being the chief exporters. Rye is particularly popular in Scandinavia, Eastern Europe and Russia. Whole or kibbled grain, flakes and flour are available. The milling process is similar to wheat. Dark rye is obtained by milling the whole rye grain, whilst light has been sifted to remove the bulk of the bran particles or by mixing dark rye with wheat flour, often desirable since rye has only a small gluten content. Consequently the extraction rate and fibre content of rye flour varies. Rye's nutritional value approximates to wheat's. Bread containing rye flour keeps moist for longer periods than white wheat bread and is traditionally made by using a sour-dough culture starter. Dark pumpernickel bread uses coarse rye meal in its production. Rye groats may be soaked and cooked like rice and are delicious as a salad combined with cubes of cooked meat/sausage, courgette, tomato and spring onion.

WHEAT

The most important grain in this country, and indeed of half the world's population, wheat was first cultivated roughly 10,000 years ago around the Eastern Mediterranean. Its nature allows it to flourish in most climates, the wheat grown in Britain being of a softer variety than the imported American, Canadian and Russian type which is high in gluten and therefore excellent for breadmaking. Wheat's versatility means that a number of different products can be obtained from the milling process, namely – bulghur, kibbled wheat, cracked wheat, flours of varying extraction rates, bran, wheatgerm and flakes. Durum wheat is excellent for making pasta, couscous and semolina.

Flour is produced by conditioning the cleaned wheat to enable easier separation of bran from the endosperm, before passing it through several sets of break rolls, which are grooved rolls, rotating in opposite directions, one faster than the other. The endosperm, which is free from the outer husk, is sieved off while the particles with skin still attached move on to the next set of break rolls. The endosperm is then milled between smooth reduction rollers and sieved to obtain fine flour. Thus the end products of the milling process are white flour (of 72-74% extraction, that is 16-18% of the wheat grain has been removed), bran and wheatgerm. For brown flour some of the bran and wheatgerm are added back to the flour, giving an extraction rate of 85-90%, while wholemeal has all of the germ and bran returned and an extraction rate of 100%. Stoneground flour is made by grinding the wheatgrain between two large, grooved, flat stones. The grain is not damaged to such an extent as during roller milling, resulting in a closer textured baked product since the gluten has not been "freed" to such an extent as when the flour has been roller milled. Since most of the nutrients in flour are stored in the germ wholemeal and brown flours are more nutritious than white, and also have a higher percentage of fibre – approximate values being 11, 8 and 3% respectively. Wholemeal and brown flour are particularly rich in iron, thiamin and nicotinic acid while, by law, calcium must be added to brown and white flour, making them richer than wholemeal in this respect, as well as iron and B vitamins to white although wholemeal and brown are still greater sources. Flour also contributes a valuable amount of protein to the diet and is predominantly a carbohydrate food. The three main types of flour (wholemeal, brown and white) are available in both plain and self-raising forms. Brown flour is particularly favourable for those who wish to increase the amount of fibre in their diet but find wholemeal gives an unacceptably heavy result. Malted wheat flour, which is basically a brown flour with added grains of wheat, which have been moistened to facilitate germination, and then roasted, is also available and can be used in a wide range of baked goods – cakes, scones, pastries, crumbles and bread. It has a distinctive nutty texture and is slightly sweet. White or wholemeal flour may also be used in its production. The colour of white flour improves naturally if it is left to mature for some time. However, under modern storing conditions, this standing period is impractical, and oxidising agents must be added to speed up this aging process. Flour which has not been bleached is available though and sold as "unbleached" flour. This is likely to have a yellow tinge.

Bran was first publicised in the 1880's by Dr. Allinson for the treatment of many diseases, and its importance as a dietary regulator is much noted today as an aid to combating the diseases of modern affluent society. Although fibre itself is indigestible the bran is rich in protein and B vitamins. Incorporated in cereals, stews, bread, cakes, biscuits and pastry bran is an important "bulking" agent, of which we are being encouraged to increase our daily intake.

Wheatgerm, the embryo of the wheat grain, provides a store of all the nutrients needed for the grain's growth – vitamin A, B group vitamins, vitamin E, iron, calcium and protein. This part of the grain harbours the fat, which although is only present in a small amount, does mean that it is prone to rancidity, however stabilised wheatgerm is available. For this reason, white flour can be stored in a cool dry place for up to 6 months, whereas wholemeal and brown flours should be used within 3 months of purchase. Wheatgerm is best kept under refrigeration. Use in the same way as bran.

Whole wheat berries are available for grinding flour at home or are excellent sprouted and used in salads.

Kibbled wheat is simply wheat grains which have been cracked in a kibbler rather than milled. The broken grains are delicious in bread, giving it a crunchiness, and also make a good gruel-like cereal. Since the pieces are smaller than whole berries they cook much quicker.

Cracked wheat is similar to kibbled wheat only the grain is put under pressure to split it.

Wheat flakes are produced by rolling whole wheat grains which may then be toasted. These can be eaten raw in muesli or used in crumble toppings and pastries.

Bulghur also known as cracked wheat or pourgouri, is a very old form of wheat used as a rice substitute in Eastern European cooking. Originally whole wheat grains were simmered until tender and left to dry in the sun before the fibrous layers were removed by dampening with water and rubbing the grains between the hands. Stones were then used to crack the grain. Nowadays bulghur is sold parboiled – the cleaned wheat having been steamed, dried, dehulled and cracked. The USA is a large producer, sending bulghur as a relief grain to countries in the Far East who face famine, since it is a way of using wheat grain to produce a food which is familiar to the native diet, bulghur being similar in nature to rice. It keeps for 6-8 months and takes about 10 minutes to cook in boiling water. Serve as a salad, stuffing for vegetables or substitute for rice, potatoes or pasta.

Durum Wheat

An amber coloured wheat berry grown mainly in North America, but also Canada, the Mediterranean, Britain and France. Durum wheat yields a strong flour.

Pasta Durum wheat provides an ideal flour for pasta making, its high gluten content ensuring that the dough holds its shape and does not disintegrate on cooking. To make wholewheat pasta the wheat is coarsely ground into semolina. Water is then added to form a dough, soft enough to be extruded through tubes to produce the desired shape. The pasta is then dried to lengthen its storage life. Dried pasta keeps for 2 years, whereas fresh must be consumed fairly quickly. Various shapes are available – macaroni, shells, lasagne (some varieties need no pre-cooking), spaghetti, tagliatelli, spirals, wheels and noodles. In addition to ordinary pasta, sieved spinach may be added to the dough, usually for lasagne and tagliatelli. High fibre spaghetti is now available, having twice as much fibre as non-wholewheat pastas, without the rough texture. Cooking times are dependant on the pasta's shape, but most tend to take 8-12 minutes. Add a drop of oil to the pan to prevent pasta sticking and allow 2-3oz (50-75g) per person. Serve curved, twisted shapes with a sauce and use tiny pasta for soups.

Semolina is the product of the break rollers and has a gritty texture since the particles are larger than when they reach the flour stage. Made from durum wheat, a wholemeal variety to which bran has been added is now available. Semolina forms the basic ingredient of gnocchi and is widely used in this country for milk puddings. Used in cakes and biscuits it gives a crunchy texture.

Couscous is essentially a pasta made from durum semolina and water which is dried and then ground. It is very popular in the Middle East where it is economically steamed over a stew/soup which is meanwhile cooking below. To cook simply sprinkle with a little water and steam for 50-60 minutes until fluffy. Traditionally couscous is served with a lamb, vegetable and chick pea stew.

Millet   Rye   Rice

Country Plait

Served hot or cold, scone dough is an ideal low fat alternative for shortcrust pastry.

Filling
>1 teasp (5ml spoon) oil
>1 small onion, thinly sliced
>3oz (75g) cooked potato, diced
>2oz (50g) sweetcorn kernels, cooked
>2 tablesps (2 × 15ml spoons) finely chopped parsley
>salt and pepper
>4oz (125g) vegetarian Cheddar, grated

Scone dough
>7oz (200g) self-raising wholemeal flour
>1oz (25g) polyunsaturated margarine
>1oz (25g) wheat, rye or barley flakes
>¼ pint (150ml) milk

Topping
>beaten egg
>grated cheese
>wheat, rye or barley flakes

19

1. Heat oil. Add onion and cook until soft, about 4-5 minutes. Remove from heat and stir in potato, sweetcorn and parsley. Season to taste.

2. For the scone: rub fat into flour until mixture resembles fine breadcrumbs. Add flakes. Stir in milk and mix to a soft dough. Turn out onto a lightly floured surface and knead gently until smooth.

3. Roll out to a square 10" × 10" (25cm × 25cm). Place potato mixture down centre third. Top with cheese and flatten slightly. Make diagonal cuts at ¾" (2cm) intervals down each side. Brush with beaten egg. Criss cross dough over filling to make a plait.

4. Place on a greased baking tray. Brush with egg and sprinkle with cheese and flakes. Bake at 200°C, 400°F, gas 6 for 25-30 minutes until golden.

Serves 4-6

Leek and Mushroom Pancake Pie

Buckwheat flour is excellent for pancake making, giving them a rich brown colour and unusual flavour. Serve this savoury layer with lightly cooked broccoli spears.

Pancake batter
3oz (75g) buckwheat flour
1oz (25g) self-raising wholemeal flour
pinch of salt
1 (size 3) egg
½ pint (300ml) skimmed milk
oil

Filling
½oz (15g) polyunsaturated margarine
12oz (350g) leeks, sliced, washed and drained
4oz (125g) button mushrooms, washed, dried and quartered
1oz (25g) wholemeal flour
¼ pint (150ml) ½ white wine, ½ milk
2 medium tomatoes, roughly chopped
3oz (75g) Cheddar cheese, grated
2oz (50g) cashew nuts, toasted and roughly chopped
salt and pepper

1. Mix flours and salt together in a bowl. Add egg and half milk, beat to a smooth batter. Gradually whisk in remaining milk. Allow to stand while preparing filling.

2. Melt margarine, add leeks and cook for 5-6 minutes, until just tender. Stir in mushrooms and continue cooking for another 2 minutes.

3. Add flour, cook for 2-3 minutes. Blend in wine and milk, bring to the boil and add tomato, 2oz (50g) cheese and 1½oz (40g) cashews. Simmer for 1-2 minutes. Season to taste.

4. Heat a little oil in a 7″ (18cm) diameter omelette pan. Pour off any excess. Spoon enough batter to just cover base into pan and cook for 1-2 minutes until set. Flip pancake over and cook until golden. Use batter to make 8 pancakes.

5. Layer pancakes with filling in a greased, ovenproof dish. Sprinkle reserved cheese and nuts over pancake, cover with foil and bake at 200°C, 400°F, gas 6 for 30-35 minutes, removing foil for last 10 minutes of cooking.

Serves 4

Orange and Watercress Bulghur Salad

Bulghur makes a filling salad, ideal during winter as an accompaniment to marinaded mushrooms or cold meats.

4oz (125g) bulghur
2 small oranges
4 tablesps (4 × 15ml spoons) oil
1 tablesp (15ml spoon) vinegar
½ teasp (2.5ml spoon) sugar
¼ teasp (1.25ml spoon) dry mustard
salt and pepper
½ bunch watercress, washed and roughly chopped
½ medium green pepper, stalk and seeds removed, thinly sliced
1oz (25g) walnuts, roughly chopped

1. Rinse bulghur. Place in a saucepan with ½ pint (300ml) water and a little salt. Bring to the boil, cover and simmer for about 10 minutes until all the liquid has been absorbed.

2. Using a sharp knife remove rind and pith from orange. Cut segments away from skin and squeeze any remaining juice from skin. Halve segments. Place juice in a bowl with oil, vinegar, sugar, mustard and seasonings. Whisk until combined.

3. Stir vinaigrette into cooked bulghur and leave until cold.

4. Toss in watercress, pepper, walnuts and orange segments.

Serves 6-8

Avocado, Chicken and Bacon Tacos

Tacos are a traditional Mexican dish – a pancake-like snack made from maize meal blended with wheat flour to give a pliable dough. They make a "fun food" for casual entertaining.

Taco shells
2oz (50g) maize meal
2oz (50g) wholemeal flour
pinch salt
3 tablesps (3 × 15ml spoons) warm water
2 tablesps (2 × 15ml spoons) corn oil

Filling
6 medium lettuce leaves, shredded
1 medium tomato, finely diced
4oz (125g) cooked chicken, diced
½ small, ripe avocado, diced
3 rashers back bacon, grilled and chopped

Dressing
5.29oz (150g) carton natural low fat yoghurt
3 tablesps (3 × 15ml spoons) tomato, chilli or barbecue relish

1. Combine, maize, wheat flour and salt in a bowl. Add water and oil and mix to a soft dough. Knead until smooth.

2. Roll out very thinly on a lightly floured surface until almost transparent. Using a 5½" (14cm) saucer as a guide cut out 6 circles, re-rolling dough as necessary.

3. Dry fry in a small frying pan for 45 seconds, flip over and continue cooking for a further 30 seconds until the pancakes lose their transparency and become flecked with brown spots. Remove from pan and fold over the handle of a large wooden spoon. Leave until cold.

4. Divide lettuce between taco shells. Sprinkle with tomato, chicken, avocado and then bacon.

5. Beat together sauce ingredients and spoon over filling. Serve at once.

Makes 6

Savoury Brown Rice with Tarragon and Lemon

Brown rice provides a moist, nutty base for this stuffing. The recipe is enough to fill 2 peppers or a small chicken. Alternatively, bake as balls to accompany lamb.

2oz (50g) brown rice
6fl oz (175ml) vegetable stock
1 teasp (5ml spoon) dried tarragon
2 teasps (2 × 5ml spoons) oil
1 small onion, finely chopped
1oz (25g) brazil nuts, thinly sliced
2oz (50g) button mushrooms, washed, dried and finely chopped
1oz (25g) raisins
finely grated rind of ½ lemon
pepper to taste
1 (size 3) egg, beaten

1. Rinse rice. Bring stock to the boil, add rice and tarragon, cover and simmer for 40-45 minutes until liquid is absorbed and rice cooked.

2. Heat oil, add onion and nuts and cook for 10 minutes. Add mushrooms and sauté for a further 5 minutes. Stir in rice, raisins, lemon rind, pepper and enough egg to bind. Use as required.

Wholewheat Pasta with Peppered Beef

This quick and easy sauce is ideal with nutty wholewheat pasta. Serve accompanied with a crisp green salad.

12oz (350g) lean minced beef
1 medium onion, chopped
1 clove garlic, crushed
2-3 tablesps (2-3 × 15ml spoons) wholemeal flour
14oz (400g) can tomatoes
¼ pint (150ml) beef stock
1 medium red pepper, stalk and seeds removed, thinly sliced
1 medium green pepper, stalk and seeds removed, thinly sliced
2 tablesps (2 × 15ml spoons) tomato purée
1 teasp (5ml spoon) dried basil
1 teasp (5ml spoon) sugar
bayleaf
salt and pepper
10oz (275g) wholewheat pasta – macaroni, spirals or shells

1. Brown meat over a high heat for 3-4 minutes. Add onion and garlic, cook for a further 4-5 minutes until softened.

2. Stir in enough flour to absorb juices and cook for 1-2 minutes. Add tomatoes, stock, peppers, tomato purée, basil, sugar and bayleaf. Bring to the boil and season to taste. Cover and simmer for 30-35 minutes.

3.   Bring a pan of salted water to the boil, add pasta and a drop of oil, stir once. Boil rapidly for 8-12 minutes until pasta is cooked but still has a slight "bite".

4.   Drain pasta and arrange in serving dish. Remove bayleaf from sauce and pour over pasta. Serve at once.

Serves 4

Lemon Rice Pudding

The gently infused lemon grass turns ordinary rice pudding into something special.

   1½oz (40g) short grain rice
   1oz (25g) soft brown sugar
   2 shoots lemon grass
   1 pint (600ml) milk

1.   Wash rice. Combine with sugar in a 1½ pint (900ml) ovenproof dish.

2.   Remove any discoloured blades from lemon grass and trim to 6" (15cm). Bruise with a knife to release lemon oils and add whole shoots to rice.

3.   Pour milk over ingredients. Bake at 150°C, 300°F, gas 2 for 2 hours. Stir once or twice during cooking.

4.   Remove lemon grass and continue cooking pudding for a further 30 minutes. Serve hot or cold.

Serves 4

Semolina Soufflé

Any variety of no added sugar jam is suitable for this special pudding, although a fruit purée could be spread over the base of the dish instead.

 2oz (50g) wholemeal semolina
 1 pint (600ml) milk
 2oz (50g) sultanas
 1oz (25g) brown sugar
 few drops vanilla essence
 2 (size 3) eggs, separated
 3 tablesps (3 × 15ml spoons) no added sugar jam, warmed
 1oz (25g) desiccated coconut

1. Preheat oven 180°C, 350°F, gas 4. Lightly grease a 2 pint (1 litre) ovenproof soufflé dish.

2. Sprinkle semolina onto milk. Bring to the boil, stirring continuously and cook for 2-3 minutes. Remove from heat. Add sultanas, sugar, essence and egg yolks.

3. Stiffly whisk whites and fold into mixture. Pour into prepared dish and level surface. Spoon melted jam over top and sprinkle with coconut. Bake for 25-30 minutes until risen. Serve at once.

Serves 8

CHAPTER 2

══ Pulses ══

Collectively known as pulses or legumes, dried peas, beans and lentils are the seeds of pod bearing plants and an inexpensive source of protein, thiamin, niacin, iron and potassium, with the added advantages of being low in fat (soya beans are the exception) and high in fibre, adding valuable bulk to the diet.

Pulses are not exploited to fulfill their potential because of the long soaking and cooking times required. This obstacle has been surmounted by the availability of a number of varieties of canned legumes (although they are more expensive than if purchased dried) which can be added directly to salads or reheated for casseroles and bakes.

Dehydrated beans and peas need to be soaked in order to reduce their cooking time and to leach out some of the toxic substances which are present and may give rise to indigestion. Lentils, on the other hand, need little or no soaking. Consequently pulses should be drained after soaking and fresh water used for cooking. Since they swell to about double their original size, 3 parts water should be added to every one of peas/beans. 2 hours is the minimum soaking time. Normally they are left overnight, which is also usually more convenient. Cold water should be used since warm conditions encourage the pulses to start fermenting and sprouting. However, if the pulses are needed at short notice then they can be brought to the boil, simmered for 2 minutes, removed from the heat and left to stand in the water for 1 hour before cooking. Grit, sticks and small stones tend to be mixed with the pulses when purchased so it is best to pick over them and then rinse thoroughly before soaking. Since a number of legumes contain poisonous substances on their skins which can cause severe stomach pains it is safest to rapidly boil all beans for 10 minutes before simmering, this way the toxins are destroyed. As regards seasoning, salt and acidic ingredients should be added right at the end of the cooking process since they toughen the skins and the pulses will never feel properly cooked. A pressure cooker enables cooking times to be dramatically reduced.

Legumes have a mealy texture making them an excellent meat or fish substitute. Served with grains to complement their amino acid content, they are a valuable source of protein, particularly for vegetarians. Allow 2oz (50g) raw, 4oz (125g) cooked pulses per person and add to soups, casseroles and salads, or use for the base of pâtés, pie fillings and patties. Legumes need generous seasoning to heighten their flavour – herbs, spices, onion and garlic all combine well.

Choose pulses which are even sized, of good colour and not wrinkled or broken. Legumes store well in a cool, dark place for up to 1 year in airtight containers, longer and they tend to toughen – in which case their cooking times will need to be increased.

Sprouting

Bean sprouts can be purchased fresh or canned and are excellent eaten raw or cooked. White shoots with yellow/green sprouts are germinated soya or mung beans. However, a much wider variety can be obtained by sprouting pulses at home. These take 5-8 days to cultivate under warm, moist conditions. Select whole pulses, split peas or lentils are not suitable, and pick over to remove all broken ones since these will not sprout. Rinse and place in a large glass jar, cover the mouth with muslin and secure. Leave jar at an angle so that it drains and rinse with warm water twice a day. Sprouts will keep for 2-3 days stored in the fridge. Wash before using and serve in a salad or toss into a stir fry dish for the last 2 minutes of cooking. Sprouted legumes are very rich in vitamin C (which is not present when they are in their dried state) since during germination some of the starch is broken down into the vitamins and minerals required for growth which takes place naturally under the conditions that encourage sprouting. Grains and seeds can also be sprouted. Alfalfa sprouts are particularly nutritious containing more protein than meat as well as being rich in vitamins and minerals. Also known as buffalo herb or lucerne, the Arabians originally fed it to their horses for its strength giving properties.

BEANS

ADUKI or ADZUKI BEAN

Also known as "Prince of the Orient", this variety is very popular in the Far East, having originated in Japan and spread to China and Korea many centuries ago. The small, oblong, reddish-brown beans are the seeds of a bushy plant and have a slightly sweet flavour. Aduki beans are particularly high in protein, calcium and iron as well as being a good source of fibre, vitamin A and the B group. Soak and cook for about 45 minutes.

28

BUTTER, SIEVA, LIMA or MADAGASCAR BEAN

Originally, as its name suggests, from Lima in Peru this variety is best known as the butter bean in Europe. Widely cultivated throughout North and South America, tropical Africa and Spain lima (sieva) beans are slightly smaller and sweeter than the oval, cream coloured, flat butterbeans which are available in canned or dried form over here. The beans take 45-50 minutes to cook and have a dry, floury texture which tends to break up easily once they are tender. Traditionally served with boiled bacon butter beans are delicious hot or cold.

BLACK-EYED BEAN

Native to Africa from where it spread to America and countries with a tropical climate black-eyed beans are associated with the South American dish of pork and candied sweet potatoes. Their flavour combines well with ham, garlic and onion. The beans are small and kidney shaped, similar to haricots in appearance, except that the creamy skin has a black spot in the inner bend of the bean, hence its name "black-eye". One of the few beans which do not need soaking black-eyed beans take 30-40 minutes to cook and have an earthy flavour.

BORLOTTI or ROSE COCOA BEAN

Belonging to the kidney bean family with the familiar shape, its colour varies from pale pink to deep pink-brown, generally the paler the better the bean. Borlotti beans have a speckled appearance and slightly sweet taste. Cook for 1 hour after soaking overnight and boiling for 10 minutes.

CANNELINI, FASIOLA or WHITE BEAN

Of the kidney bean family this bean is longer than most varieties and plump but thin. Soak, boil and cook for 1-1½ hours until tender. Use cannelini beans in bakes, salads and casseroles, or serve as a side dish tossed in garlic and fresh herbs.

FIELD BEAN

Small, dark brown and round this bean is native to England and grows in northern climates. It has an earthy flavour and requires 1 hour's cooking.

FLAGEOLET BEAN

Very popular in France and Italy, flageolets are pale green or white, elongated, narrow in width but plump. Soak, boil and cook for 1¼ hours.

HARICOT or NAVY BEAN

More familiar as baked beans in tomato sauce, haricot beans belong to the kidney bean family. They are small and white, delicious added to soups and stews, and the traditional bean used for cassoulet. Soak, boil and cook for 1¼ hours.

KIDNEY BEAN

Red kidney beans are the most common, although black ones are available. Kidney beans are especially popular in Mexico, where they are an essential ingredient of chilli con carne, and in Central and South America. The red beans have pale pink flesh and must be soaked and then boiled for 10 minutes before simmering for a further 50 minutes. The black beans are widely used in Caribbean cookery and can be substituted for red ones in recipes, but take longer to cook. As with other dried beans they are a particularly good source of protein, fibre, vitamins A and the B group, calcium and iron. There are many varieties of kidney beans which may be cultivated for their dried seeds or fresh pods (such as French beans). Records of kidney beans growing in North America date back to prehistoric times.

MUNG BEAN, GREEN, GOLDEN or BLACK GRAM

First cultivated in India this bean is popular throughout Asia. The tiny, oblong, olive green legume has pale yellow flesh and takes ½ hour to cook whole, 15 minutes if split. The green variety is commonly used for sprouting. Mung beans have the highest vitamin A content of all dried legumes.

PINTO BEAN

These are plump, brown and speckled and turn pink on cooking. Soak, boil and simmer for 1 hour.

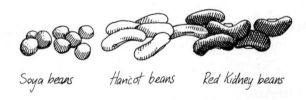

Soya beans   Haricot beans   Red Kidney beans

SOYA BEAN

The most versatile pulse, and richest in protein, soya beans are aptly called "the meat of the earth" in the Far East, from whence they originated. Records of their use in China date back 4,000 years after which the bean spread to Korea and Japan. The 1940's saw a surge in the use of soya and today it is the USA who lead world cultivation. The annual, bushy, soya bean plants require a humid climate to bear their pods containing three beans which ripen to a golden colour when fully mature. Black soya beans which are actually dark brown are less common in this country than the larger, yellow, rounded variety. Nutritionally the beans are a valuable source of protein – containing more than is found in meat, fish and eggs – the protein, unlike with the other pulses, is made up of all eight essential amino acids which the body cannot manufacture. However, soya is also comparatively high in fat for a legume, although this has advantages in the production of the by product, oil. Soya beans are a good source of easily assimilated iron, calcium, vitamin A and niacin as well as containing lecithin and linoleic acid which help to reduce the level of cholesterol in the blood. Soya beans take 2 hours to cook after overnight soaking, whereas cracked beans take only 45 minutes and tend to cook down to a pulp.

The reason for the soya bean's popularity lies in the diverse products which can be obtained from it:

Soya flour is yellow in colour and used to thicken soups, gravies and casseroles. Commercially it is favoured by bakers as an improver of texture and for extending a product's shelf life. Basically there are three types available:

  a) full fat flour, which contains 20% fat
  b) medium fat flour, which contains 5-8% fat
  c) fat-free flour.

Consequently, when using, the amounts of liquid added will have to be modified accordingly since medium fat and fat-free flours require more liquid than full fat. Soya flour does not contain gluten and is therefore unsuitable for use on its own in bread making. To obtain the flour the cleaned soya beans are cooked, dried, hulled and then ground to produce full fat flour, which contains 40% protein. De-fatted flour has had the oil extracted by a crushing process after the beans have been hulled, and contains 50% protein.

Soya flakes are produced after hulling and can be used in place of oats, barley, rye or wheat flakes in muesli and baked goods.

Soya oil is extracted from flour or flakes to produce salad oil, cooking shortening or margarine. Soya oil is either obtained by the expeller process – where the cooked beans are pressed so that the oil is released – or through the use of solvents to separate chemically the oil from the flour.

Textured vegetable protein (TVP) is one of the wonders of modern technology where what originally started as a bean is transformed into a product similar in flavour and texture to meat, only much less expensive, making it an ideal protein substitute. TVP can be manufactured by extrusion or spinning. The spun variety is more expensive but has a realistic fibrous texture. Soya protein isolate is spun in a similar way to textile fibres to achieve the structure of meat. The extrusion process involves making the de-fatted soya flour concentrate into a dough with colourings and flavourings and forcing it through a steam chamber fitted with the required shape and size nozzle. Hence chunks or granules are obtained which are reconstituted when required for use in sausage and burger mixes, meat loaves, curries and casseroles.

Tofu is a soya bean curd which is widely used in Chinese and Japanese cooking and known as "the meat without bones". Similar in appearance and texture to a soft cheese it is added towards the end of cooking since due to its delicate texture it tends to break up easily. It does not in fact need to be cooked, and because of its mild flavour is suitable for both sweet and savoury dishes. Uses include low fat salad dressings, stir-fried vegetable dishes (instead of adding meat), cheesecake fillings and creamy desserts. Tofu is made from soya beans which have been cooked, puréed and then strained. The liquid (curd) is set using coagulants, as for cheese making. Hence it is low in fibre and fat, but high in protein. Firm or soft tofu, depending on the degree of pressing, is available. Silken tofu, a blend of soya curds and whey has a smooth texture and is consequently more suited for use where a creamy texture is required. Purchased fresh or long life, tofu is usually sold pasteurised in vacuum packs and should be kept refrigerated.*

Soya milk is available in various forms – powdered, concentrated or long-life. It has less calories than full fat and semi-skimmed cow's milk and more iron, however, it is not such a good source of calcium, phosphorus or vitamin A. The milk is ideal for those who are allergic to cow's milk and for vegans. It has a rich, creamy taste and is delicious in sauces, flan fillings, and wherever cow's milk would normally be used. The manufacturing process is the same as for tofu except that the milk is not set.

32

Soy sauce is the product of soya beans which have been cooked, mixed with roasted wheat and then treated with a micro-organism. Salt is added to speed up the fungus' growth, and after a fermentation period the rich, brown liquid is strained off and bottled. Light and the more concentrated dark soy sauce are available and can be used in a similar way to Worcestershire sauce.

Miso is a salty paste similar in texture to smooth peanut butter. A Japanese product miso is made from fermented soya beans. Added to stews, sauces, soups and pâtés, it is an excellent flavouring for meatless dishes. Tamari is the liquid produced during the manufacture of miso.

*Tofu can be frozen but tends to toughen on defrosting.

LENTILS

Originally cultivated in the East and introduced into America at the beginning of this century. Of the pulses lentils are second only in protein to soya beans. They come in many shapes and sizes, but can basically be divided into whole or split. Neither type need soaking. Green lentils are relatively large, disc-shaped and olive green in colour. These take 45 minutes to cook. Brown lentils are slightly smaller and require 10 minutes less cooking. Both these are whole and hold their shape when cooked making them a suitable alternative to rice. Mix with vegetables and dress with a vinaigrette. Split lentils are bright orange in colour, smaller and form a purée on cooking. These are therefore more suitable as a thickener in soups, stews and patties.

PEAS

Whole or split yellow or green peas are available. The split ones having had their skins removed and needing 30-40 minutes, as opposed to 1½ hours for whole peas, to cook. Add a bouquet garni, chopped onion and some bacon to the cooking liquor for flavour. Peas contribute fibre and protein to stews and soups.

Split Peas and Lentils

CHICK PEA, BENGAL GRAM (INDIA), EGYPTIAN PEA or GARBANZO PEA (USA and SPAIN)

Thought to have originated in Western Asia the peas are now grown commercially in America, Africa and Australia. In Mediterranean countries chick peas are ground and mixed with garlic, oil and lemon juice to make hummous, classically served with pitta bread. Whereas in North Africa a flour is made from the peas which is used for couscous as an alternative to using durum wheat. White, black, brown and red varieties are available in addition to the golden coloured type common in this country. The size of a hazelnut they have a distinctive hook at each end, are wrinkled in appearance and have a floury taste. Chick peas contain more vitamin C and provide double the usual amount of iron than most legumes. They will take between 1-1½ hours to cook after soaking.

Chick Peas

GRAM (BESAN) FLOUR

A fine, light weight, golden flour with a slightly gritty texture. Gram flour is milled from dehusked split yellow dāl (split peas) and is traditionally used in Indian cookery for fritter batters or combined with chapatti flour to make chapatties. Mix gram flour with wheat flour to make shortcrust pastry with a crumbly texture and rich colour. Nutritionally gram flour contains a higher percentage of protein, fat, fibre, calcium and iron than wheat flours.

CAROB BEAN

Although technically a pulse the carob bean is not used in the same way. Originally from Syria and Palestine the tree was introduced into Greece from whence it spread to Italy and is now also grown in many countries with a Mediterranean climate – including Spain, Portugal, North Africa and South America. Carob beans are the fruit of the evergreen tree which is able to grow on the poorest of soils to a height between 36ft-60ft (12m-20m). The leathery pods are the size of a flat, wizened, dark chocolate coloured banana, varying from 4"-14" (10cm-35cm) in length. Records of the carob tree's existence date back to the Bible – the pig's husks eaten by the prodigal son were probably carob pods. Each pod bears up to 15 red-brown seeds, so uniform in size that they were the original measure for the "carat" weight. As interest in the use of the pulp as a substitute for cocoa grows more trees are being specially cultivated to yield higher grade beans. The beans fall to the ground when ripe and are left to dry in the sun before being taken to the factory for cleaning. The brittle pods are then broken up, at which stage the seeds are removed and made into a powdered gum which is used commercially as a stabiliser and emulsifier. The carob pulp is roasted to develop its flavour and colour before being milled and sieved to give a powder, slightly lighter in appearance than cocoa. Nutritionally it is lower in fat than cocoa but higher in sugar. Calorific wise carob is marginally lower. Carob has five times more iron than cocoa, which is itself regarded as a rich source of this nutrient, contains more calcium and a small amount of vitamins A, D and the B group. Carob powder is free from the stimulants caffeine and theobromine and migraine causing substances. It also has anti-diarrhetic properties. Roughly half the price of cocoa, carob can be used as a substitute in drinks, cakes, biscuits, sauces and puddings. Carob confectionary bars, made in a similar way to chocolate, are also available either plain or in a range of flavours such as orange, mint, fruit and nut. A no added sugar version can also be found – mainly in health food shops or large chemists. Carob flavoured soya milk based drinks as well as powdered carob based beverages are becoming more popular. See also "Beverages and Juices" chapter.

Bierwurst with Beans

A quick, all-in-one bean dish. Use any kind of cooked spicy sausage if bierwurst is unavailable.

6oz (175g) black-eyed beans
8oz (225g) French or Kenya beans, topped and tailed and sliced into 1½" (4cm) lengths
salt
½oz (15g) polyunsaturated margarine
1 onion, thinly sliced
1 clove garlic, crushed
8oz (225g) bierwurst sausage, diced
½ teasp (2.5ml spoon) dried basil
pepper

1. Wash and drain black-eyed beans and green beans. Place black-eyed beans in a pan with plenty of water. Bring to the boil, cover and simmer for 30 minutes.

2. Add green beans and season with salt. Cook for a further 6-8 minutes.

3. Melt margarine. Add onion and garlic, fry for 5 minutes. Stir in sausage, herb and pepper to taste. Continue cooking for 5 minutes.

4. Drain beans and add to sausage mixture. Stir until thoroughly combined and heated through. Serve hot.

Serves 4

Tofu in Barbecue Sauce

This barbecue sauce is also delicious used as a coating for chicken drumsticks or brushed onto chops before grilling.

Sauce

4 tablesps (4 × 15ml spoons) water
2 tablesps (2 × 15ml spoons) soft brown sugar
2 tablesps (2 × 15ml spoons) wine vinegar
2 tablesps (2 × 15ml spoons) tomato purée
1 tablesp (15ml spoon) Worcestershire sauce
1 tablesp (15ml spoon) soy sauce
1 teasp (5ml spoon) paprika
½ teasp (2.5ml spoon) mustard powder

Remaining ingredients

10oz (283.5g) packet firm tofu, washed and cut into ½" (12.5mm) cubes
4 teasps (4 × 5ml spoons) vegetable oil
3oz (75g) baby sweetcorn, washed and cut into ½" (12.5mm) lengths
1 medium red pepper, stalk and seeds removed, cut into ½" (12.5mm) cubes
8oz (225g) courgettes, wiped and thinly sliced
4 large spring onions, trimmed and thinly sliced
6oz (175g) beansprouts, washed

1. Mix together all sauce ingredients. Add cubed tofu and leave to marinate for at least 2 hours, stirring occasionally.

2. Heat 3 teaspoons (3 × 5ml spoons) oil in a large frying pan. Add sweetcorn and cook over a moderate heat for 5 minutes.

3. Stir in pepper, courgette and onion with remaining oil and continue to cook for 5 minutes.

4. Add beansprouts and cook for 2-3 minutes. Stir in tofu with sauce. Bring to the boil and simmer for 5 minutes until heated through. Serve at once.

Serves 4

Cheesey Topped Lentil Bake

Superb with a crisp green salad for everyday eating. Lentils, being high in protein, make an excellent meat replacement.

2 teasps (2 × 5ml spoons) oil
1 large onion, chopped
1 large clove garlic, crushed
6oz (175g) red split lentils, washed and drained
14oz (400g) can tomatoes
¾ pint (450ml) vegetable stock
6oz (175g) flat mushrooms, washed, dried and thickly sliced
2 medium carrots, peeled and sliced into rings
1 teasp (5ml spoon) dried mixed herbs
salt and paprika

Cheese custard

½ pint (300ml) milk
2 (size 3) eggs, beaten
3oz (75g) low fat Cheddar cheese, grated
½ teasp (2.5ml spoon) mustard
salt and pepper

1. Heat oil, add onion and garlic and cook for 5 minutes.

2. Stir in lentils, tomatoes and stock, bring to the boil and boil rapidly for 10 minutes, stirring occasionally to prevent lentils from sticking.

3. Add mushrooms, carrots and herbs, cover and simmer for 20-25 minutes, removing lid for last 5-10 minutes to allow the liquid to evaporate. Season to taste with salt and paprika. Pour into a 2¾ pint (1.6 litre) ovenproof dish.

4. Beat together milk, eggs, cheese, mustard and seasoning. Pour over lentil mixture and bake at 180°C, 350°F, gas 4 for 30-40 minutes until golden and set.

Serves 6.

Spicy Indian Lamb

Chick peas, flavoured with carrots, onion and mushrooms, form an authentic "mealy" base to this Indian style dish. A quick tomato sauce to accompany can be made by simmering a 14oz (400g) can plum tomatoes with 2oz (50g) finely chopped onion, ¾ pint (450ml) meat stock, bouquet garni bag, a pinch of salt, ground ginger and pepper, for 30 minutes, before thickening with 1 tablesp (15ml spoon) cornflour mixed to a smooth paste with 2 tablesps (2 × 15ml spoons) of the tomato liquid, and simmered for 2-3 minutes.

6oz (175g) dried chick peas
2 teasps (2 × 5ml spoons) vegetable oil
2oz (50g) onion, finely chopped
1 clove garlic, crushed
4oz (125g) carrots, grated
2oz (50g) flat mushrooms, finely chopped
2 tablesps (2 × 15ml spoons) milk
seeds of 4 green cardamon pods, crushed
¼ teasp (1.25ml spoon) cumin powder
salt and paprika
2 ½lb (1.1kg) leg of lamb
fat for roasting
½ teasp (2.5ml spoon) ground coriander

1. Soak chick peas overnight in plenty of cold water. Drain. Place in a pan with water to cover, bring to the boil, cover and simmer for 45 minutes until tender. Drain.

2. Heat oil. Add onion and garlic and cook until golden, about 10 minutes. Place in a blender/processor with chick peas, carrot, mushrooms, milk, crushed cardamon, cumin, salt and paprika. Blend until smooth. Allow to cool.

3. Cut bone from leg of lamb. Use about $\frac{1}{3}$ of chick pea mixture to stuff lamb. Sew up meat, reforming the original leg shape. Place remaining stuffing in a small shallow dish and cover with a piece of greased foil.

4. Place a little fat in a roasting pan and heat in oven, 200°C, 400°F, gas 6 for about 5 minutes.

5. Sprinkle lamb with coriander, add to pan and cook for 20 minutes. Reduce oven temperature to 180°C, 350°F, gas 4 and cook for a further 1¼ hours. Place remaining stuffing in oven 25 minutes before end of cooking time.

Serves 6.

Melted Cheese and Courgette Flan

Gruyere cheese can equally well be used in this recipe. Serve with a mixed bean salad and jacket potato, or cold as part of a packed meal.

Pastry
2oz (50g) gram/besan flour
2oz (50g) wholemeal flour
pinch salt
2oz (50g) white vegetable fat
2 tablesps (2 × 15ml spoons) cold water

Filling
6oz (175g) courgettes, wiped and sliced
1 small onion, peeled and thinly sliced
4oz (125g) Emmental cheese, grated
2 (size 3) eggs, beaten
¼ pint (150ml) milk
½ teasp (2.5ml spoon) mustard
salt and pepper

1. Rub fat into flours and salt. Add enough water to bind. Turn out onto a lightly floured surface and knead gently until smooth. Wrap and chill in fridge for 15-20 minutes.

2. Roll out pastry and use to line a 7" (18cm) flan ring.

3. Blanch courgette and onion in boiling water for 2 minutes. Drain well and scatter over base of flan with cheese. Beat together eggs, milk, mustard and seasoning. Pour into flan case and bake at 200°C, 400°F, gas 6 for 25-30 minutes.

Serves 4.

Rich Plum Shortcake

An upside down plum pudding combining soya flour with wheat flour to give a soft textured, rich shortcake.

1 tablesp (15ml spoon) Demerara sugar
12oz (350g) red eating plums, halved and stoned
2oz (50g) polyunsaturated margarine
1oz (25g) soft brown sugar
1 (size 3) egg, beaten
1½oz (40g) soya flour
1½oz (40g) wholemeal flour
½ teasp (2.5ml spoon) cinnamon

1. Sprinkle Demerara sugar over base of a greased 8" (20cm) round sandwich tin.

2. Arrange plums, cut side down, over base.

3. Cream fat a sugar until light and fluffy. Gradually beat in egg followed by flours and cinnamon.

4. Smooth mixture over fruit and level surface. Bake at 180°C, 350°F, gas 4 for 35 minutes until golden. Turn out and serve warm or cold.

Serves 6.

Gooseberry Fool

A special fool made with creamy soya milk, "fluffed up" with whisked egg-whites to give a light as air result.

3oz (75g) sugar
1lb (450g) gooseberries
1 (size 3) egg
1 (size 3) egg yolk
½ pint (300ml) soya milk
¼ teasp (1.25ml spoon) vanilla essence

1. Dissolve 1oz (25g) sugar in 2 tablespoons (2 × 15ml spoons) water. Add gooseberries, bring to the boil, cover and simmer for 5-10 minutes until just soft. Drain and allow to cool. Purée and sieve.

2. Whisk remaining sugar with whole egg and yolk until thick and light.

3. Heat soya milk with essence until almost boiling, remove from heat and pour onto whisked mixture. Return to heat and cook for 3-4 minutes, without boiling until custard thickens and just coats the back of a wooden spoon. (Use a double saucepan if possible).

4. Whisk together fruit purée and custard, cover and chill.

Serves 4-6.

Banana and Carob Crunch Flan

Alternatively use the carob flan case filled with halved strawberries to make a delicious pudding in the summer months.

Base
60g bar plain carob
1oz (25g) polyunsaturated margarine
4oz (125g) unsweetened muesli

Filling
2 tablesps (2 × 15ml spoons) orange juice
2 teasps (2 × 5ml spoons) powdered gelatine
2 small bananas
½ teasp (2.5ml spoon) lemon juice
5.29oz (150g) carton natural low fat yoghurt
1 tablesp (15ml spoon) clear honey

1.   Place carob and margarine in a pan and heat gently until just melted. Stir in muesli and press into base and sides of a 7″ (18cm) flan ring. Chill until firm.

2.   Dissolve gelatine in orange juice. Allow to cool slightly.

3.   Mash bananas with lemon juice. Mix in yoghurt and honey. Whisk in gelatine. Pour into flan case and chill until set.

4.   Ease flan out of ring and serve.

Serves 6.

CHAPTER 3

━━━━━ Nuts and Seeds ━━━━━

NUTS

Nuts are a versatile, high protein food. Many varieties are now widely available, conveniently shelled and ready to use, and although their textures vary only slightly there are subtle differences in flavour. Nuts have an edible kernel and hard brittle shell.

Nutritionally they are rich in protein and thus an important meat substitute for vegetarians, but also have a high fat content with a correspondingly high calorific value, chestnuts being the exception. However, they are rich in linoleic acid which has the ability to control cholesterol levels in the blood. The quantity of fibre varies with each kind of nut but overall the values are high. They also contribute useful amounts of minerals and some B vitamins to the diet. Thus, provided they are incorporated into a dish, rather than nibbled in between meals, their nutritional value can be channelled into good use.

Nuts are particularly popular because of the crunchy texture which they impart to sweet or savoury dishes. However their expense, due to importation levies and the amount of preparation required in shelling – many varieties are now sold shelled and have been roasted in order to bring out their flavour, and in some cases are salted – often deters full use being made of them. Eaten whole, nibbed, flaked or ground, nuts can be used in baking, for muesli mixes and snacks. Unshelled they will keep for about 2 years, since air, light, heat and moisture are excluded, otherwise store in an airtight container for up to 6 months in a cool, dark place.

CASHEW

Derived from its ancient name, "acajou" the pear-cashew variety is the most common and is now grown in a number of tropical regions, although originally cashews came from Brazil. India is the largest exporter. The green nut grows at the base of a red apple-like fruit (which is made into liqueur) on the tropical cashew tree. They are lightly roasted, to destroy the skin irritant present in the fleshy part around the kernel – known as the "cashew-pear" – before the nut can be shelled. The beans are white and kidney shaped with a delicate sweet flavour. Sold salted, cashews are a rich protein snack, but also high in fat. Add

43

unsalted nuts to curries, incorporate into pastry and sweet dishes or use in a savoury pancake filling – see page 20.

CHESTNUT

Not to be confused with the inedible horse chestnut, each prickly shell, which turns from green to brown as it ripens, contains 2-3 sweet chestnuts. Native to the Mediterranean they subsequently spread to North America and Southern Europe. A member of the oak and beech family chestnuts will grow in England but need a warmish climate to ripen. Many are imported fresh from Spain, available from October – January, choose plump nuts with shiny shells. Imported from France canned, whole and puréed chestnuts can be obtained all year round. Marron glacés – chestnuts cooked and preserved in syrup are also available. Dried chestnuts can be purchased from health food and speciality shops but require soaking overnight before cooking. The shiny teak-like skins of fresh chestnuts are best removed by scoring the domed face with a sharp knife and then roasting in a hot oven 200°C, 400°F, gas 6 for 15 minutes or until the skins split. Cool slightly, shell and cook for a further 45 minutes in simmering water, or roast. The nuts may then be used whole as a garnish, chopped in stuffings, puréed for soup or blended with confectioners custard and sweetened for cake or choux bun fillings. Chestnuts combine particularly well with poultry and during the winter with sprouts. Italians grind the nuts down to a creamy coloured flour which is used in breadmaking or a slightly sweet flavoured gruel. Blanched chestnuts may be frozen, otherwise keep unshelled chestnuts refrigerated for up to two months. Chestnuts have a sweet, floury taste when cooked. Consisting of about 50% water they are consequently lower in calories than most nuts and their high carbohydrate and sugar content, together with low percentage of protein and fat, makes their nutritional value an exception to the rule of this group. Chestnuts are a fairly good source of dietary fibre.

COCONUT

Malayan in origin coconut palms are now found growing wild along the Pacific and Indian shores. Known as "the tree of heaven" or "the tree of life", because of the multitudinous uses the natives put it to – including building houses with the trunks while the palm leaves provide the thatching. Ropes and mats are made from the husk and tooth picks from the veins of the leaves. While the flesh plays a valuable part in the diet oil is extracted from the dried pulp.

Fresh coconuts bought in this country have had the smooth outer skin removed to leave a thick, fibrous, rough brown husk, varying in shape between round and oval. Three indentations at one end, the "eyes" are the coconut's Achilles' heel and by puncturing two of them the clear coconut water can be drained off before splitting the kernel open to reveal ½" (12.5mm) of crisp, sweet white flesh. The water is delicious drunk on its own – when buying coconuts shake them first to ensure that the liquid has not dried up, since the amount of milk decreases as the coconut ages, and the chances are that if there is none left the coconut is an old one and the flesh likely to be dry. Eaten raw, grated coconut flesh can be added to recipes imparting an unique flavour to sweet and savoury dishes.

Desiccated coconut – this is the dried kernel of the coconut palm which has been grated into "rice" sized pieces. Since it is dehydrated it stores well in an air tight container. Desiccated coconut has a higher nutritional value than fresh. Compared with other nuts it is fairly high in calories and fat (most of which is, uncharacteristically for nuts, saturated). However, it is a good source of iron and nicotinic acid and extremely high in fibre. Coconut in this form adds flavour and texture to biscuits, cakes and puddings. Try toasting desiccated or flaked coconut and adding to muesli. A substitute for coconut milk can easily be made at home by pouring ½ pint (300ml) boiling water onto 2oz (50g) coconut and leaving it to infuse for 10 minutes before straining off the liquid.

Creamed coconut – for centuries this has been made in the tropics by pouring hot water over freshly grated coconut flesh and then squeezing the coconut by hand to extract as much of the liquid as possible. The resulting coconut cream is then blended into a variety of dishes, a favourite of the islands being a marinade for fresh fish. Packet creamed coconut is made by milling desiccated coconut to a homogeneous pulp. A substantial amount of creamed coconut is imported from Sri Lanka. Creamed coconut has a rich, sweet flavour which is ideal for sweet and sour dishes and has the characteristic of thickening on cooking. Simply dissolve the required quantity into the dish instead of using desiccated coconut. Add to curries, casseroles or sweet sauces.

Coconut oil – extracted from the dried flesh of the kernel, which is composed of approximately 50% fat, coconut oil, unlike other vegetable oils, is very high in saturated fats. Since it is solid at room temperature the majority is used for commercial applications.

MACADAMIA or QUEENSLAND NUT

These round, hard shelled nuts have a delicious flavour. Native to Australia they are also grown in Hawaii and are particularly popular in

America. Macadamias are low in protein, only contain a trace of fibre and are composed of almost 75% fat. Usually sold shelled, roasted and salted, they are expensive and consequently tend to be just handed round as cocktail nuts.

PEANUT, MONKEY-NUT, EARTH-NUT or GROUND-NUT

Peanuts are not true nuts, but the seed of a leguminous plant. The nuts actually grow in the soil. The pods, which are attached to the plant's long tendrils can be harvested after four months. Evidence of the existence of these nuts in South America dates back to 950 BC from whence explorers gradually introduced them to East Africa and the Philippines. Now peanuts are found in most countries with a hot climate, India, China and America being the largest producers. The skittle-shaped, straw-coloured brittle pod contains two nuts with red/brown skins. The skins are easily discarded by heating the nuts in a hot oven and then rubbing them off with a teatowel. Peanuts are high in calories, being comprised of 45-50% fat, but are an excellent source of protein, making them a valuable meat substitute since they contain all the essential amino acids. They are also rich in iron and nicotinic acid. Peanuts are most popular served roasted and salted as a snack, or ground and mixed with a little oil and salt for peanut butter spread. This can easily be made in the home and the crunchiness controlled to personal preference by the degree of processing. On a commercial basis oil is extracted from the nuts for use in cooking and salads. The nuts themselves are delicious in sweet or savoury recipes – biscuits, nut roasts and crumbles.

PECAN

Cultivated in North America pecan nuts have a smooth, glossy, oblong, brittle pod, which is reddish-brown in colour. The nut is formed in two halves – similar to an elongated walnut (which it is related to) in appearance but with a butterscotch flavour superior to that of walnuts. Best known for its role as the basic ingredient of American pecan pie pecans can be substituted in any recipes calling for walnuts, but because of their higher price are not as widely used.

PINE NUT, PIGNOLI or INDIAN NUT

These are the edible seeds of the stone variety of pine, native to Italy, although they are now cultivated throughout the Mediterranean where they are widely used in cooking. The tough, ridged, outer cone casing protects the delicate, long, creamy kernels which taper to a point at one end. Pine nuts are always sold as kernels since they must be matured in order to eliminate the turpentine flavour otherwise peculiar to them. Cooking is another way to dispel this disagreeable taste. Pine nuts have a slightly greasy mouth feel and their own distinctive taste. They are excellent toasted, mixed with chopped spring onion and sprinkled on cherry tomatoes with a vinaigrette to make a refreshing summer salad. Alternatively use in stuffings or mix with rice. The kernels are particularly popular in Italian cooking and are the basic ingredient of pesto – a spaghetti sauce made with garlic, fresh basil, oil and salt. As with most other nuts pine kernels are an excellent source of protein, containing about 30%, and are almost 50% fat.

PISTACHIO

Primarily grown in the Middle East (Turkey, Syria and Israel) and Greece, pistachios are also found in other Asian and Mediterranean countries as well as America. The seed, comparable to a small olive in size and shape, grows on a tree which is native to Syria. Records of their use date back to 10,000 BC. Pistachios have smooth, brittle, grey-brown shells which split when ripe to reval the nut – a green kernel shrouded with purple-yellow, thin, wrinkled skin. This is most easily removed by blanching the shelled nut, which also has the effect of heightening its natural brilliant green pigment. Both shelled and unshelled nuts can be bought, the former being best stored in a dark, airtight container to preserve the nut's colour. A relatively expensive nut, pistachios are used in confectionery – particularly Turkish delight and halva. They make an excellent decoration for puddings and cakes and impart a special flavour to ice cream. Pistachio nuts are a rich source of iron.

TIGER NUT or EARTH ALMOND

Small, shrivelled, bullet-like nuts these are the rhizomes of an African plant. Sold dried, a hint of almond can be detected in their flavour. Add to salads or grind and use in a nut loaf.

SEEDS

Often added to a dish because of their texture or to give an attractive finish – such as sprinkling on breads – seeds are also very nutritious. The germs of flowering plants they store all the nutrients required for it's growth – protein, fat, minerals and vitamins. Each variety of edible seeds have their own unique flavour which is enhanced by toasting. Their crunchy texture makes them ideal for nibbling on their own and for crumble toppings, muesli and baked goods. In a puréed form they make a delicious spread or salad dressing.

POPPY

Originally from the Middle East poppy seeds were used by the Egyptians as long ago as 1,500 BC. The opium poppy plants bear mauve or white flowers, the opium drug is extracted before the plants reach maturity, thus ensuring that the ripened seeds do not contain any habit-forming alkaloids. White or blue/grey seeds are available, the latter being referred to as "blue moon seeds" in some countries. The tiny seeds have a crunchy texture and nutty flavour. Widely used in Jewish and Indian cookery they are especially popular in breads, cakes, pastries and biscuits. Oil accounts for 40-55% of the poppy seed's weight. Popular in French cooking the oil is seldom found in this country.

PUMPKIN –see "Vegetables" chapter.

SESAME

Also known as "benne seeds", sesame seeds are looked upon as a symbol of immortality in the East since, according to Hindu mythology, they were blessed by the Gods. Indeed the Greeks, Egyptians, Persians and Hebrews have utilised the seed as a food and source of oil for thousands of years. Originally native to India the annual plant grows on poor soil in tropical and subtropical climates. Africa, Asia and South America are the main areas of cultivation with China and India being the most important producers. Sesame plants have to be resown each year. The pink, trumpet-shaped flowers mature into seed-bearing pods. White or brown-black in colour, the paler seeds are more common in this country. They are comprised of about 50% fat, hence their value as a source of oil, very high in protein and rich in B vitamins, niacin in particular, and minerals – especially calcium and iron. A popular paste used in Turkey and Arabia is tahini, made from ground sesame seeds which can be flavoured with garlic and lemon juice to make a delicious spread. Alternatively use in dips or heat and serve as a sauce. This paste can be made at home in a liquidiser or processor and used in a similar way or incorporated into sweet or savoury biscuits. Another major use is for the traditional Middle Eastern halva (halvah) sweet which is often flavoured with pistachios or vanilla. Sesame seeds add flavour to breads, biscuits, cakes and muesli. Alternatively sprinkle on rolls for a crunchy topping. The seeds are also delicious in salads. Stored in an airtight container in a cool, dry place sesame seeds will keep for 6 months.

SUNFLOWER

Originally sunflower seeds were cultivated in America by the Indians, in particular around Mexico, Peru and the North, where they were valued for their medicinal properties. Today America and Russia are the largest producers, although the plants are also widespread in Italy and Poland. The enormous flower heads which can measure more than 12" (30cm) across consist of a nucleus of hundreds of closely packed seeds surrounded by yellow petals. Varieties may be produced specifically for human consumption or for the extraction of oil. The seeds are either sold shelled or with their inedible streaked grey/cream outer husk still intact. Rich in vitamins, particularly the B group and vitamin E, iron, calcium and the trace elements the kernels are 25% protein. Sunflower seeds are valuable supplements to the diet incorporated toasted in salads, muesli and breads, eaten as a "nibble", ground into a spread or used for the manufacture of oil.

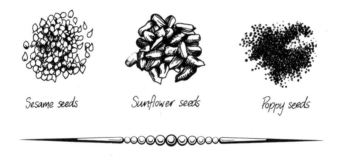

Sesame seeds   Sunflower seeds   Poppy seeds

Pine Nut and Aubergine Dip

Pine nuts give a sweetish flavour to this dip which contrasts with the lemon juice to give it "zip". It can also be used as a sandwich filling with lettuce.

1lb (450g) aubergines, wiped
3 tablesps (3 × 15ml spoons) vegetable oil
1 medium onion, chopped
1 clove garlic, crushed
2oz (50g) pine nuts, toasted
2 tablesps (2 × 15ml spoons) lemon juice
salt and pepper
chopped parsley to garnish

49

1. Pierce aubergines with a fork and place on a baking tray. Bake at 190°C, 375°F, gas 5 for 45 minutes until tender. Cool slightly and scrape out flesh.

2. Heat 1 tablesp (15ml spoon) oil. Add onion and garlic and cook for 10 minutes until soft.

3. Place in a blender with aubergine flesh, pine nuts and lemon juice. Purée until smooth.

4. Gradually add remaining oil, season to taste and chill. Garnish with parsley just before serving.

Makes ¾ pint (450ml)

Blue Moon Rolls

These enriched yeasted crescents, speckled with poppy seeds and flavoured with cheese taste good enough to eat on their own. Cut each dough circle into 12 for dinner rolls or 8 if they are to be filled.

Batter
1 tablesp (15ml spoon) dried yeast and 1 teasp (5ml spoon) sugar
or 1oz (25g) fresh yeast
6fl oz (175ml) hand hot milk
4oz (125g) strong white flour

Dough
12oz (350g) strong white flour
1 teasp (5ml spoon) salt
2oz (50g) polyunsaturated margarine
2 (size 3) eggs, beaten

Additional ingredients
4oz (125g) low fat Cheddar cheese, grated
1 tablesp (15ml spoon) poppy seeds
1 (size 4) egg, beaten
grated cheese and poppy seeds for garnish

1. Sprinkle dried yeast and sugar over milk and leave for 5 minutes. Alternatively dissolve fresh yeast in milk. Stir in flour and allow to stand for 20 minutes until frothy.

2. Rub fat into flour and salt. Stir yeast liquid and eggs into dry ingredients and form into a soft dough. Knead for about 10 minutes until smooth. Place in a greased polythene bag and leave in a warm place until doubled in size.

3. Preheat oven 200°C, 400°F, gas 6. Grease 2 baking trays.

4. Knead cheese and poppy seeds into dough until evenly incorporated. Divide in half and roll out each on a lightly floured surface to a circle, 12" (30cm) in diameter. Brush with egg and cut into 8 or 12 triangles. Roll up from the long edge and curve ends inwards to form a crescent. Place on prepared trays, brush with egg, cover and leave in a warm place for about ½ hour until doubled in size.

5. Sprinkle rolls with a little extra cheese and seeds. Bake for 20 minutes until golden. Cool on a wire rack. Serve warm or cold.

Makes 16-24

Cashew and Vegetable Ragout

A delicious vegetarian casserole, serve with jacket potatoes or rice. Vary the vegetables according to those available at the time of making.

2 tablesps (2 × 15ml spoons) vegetable oil
4oz (125g) cashew nuts
1 medium onion, thinly sliced
1 clove garlic, crushed
1 teasp (5ml spoon) paprika
1 teasp (5ml spoon) ground coriander
½ teasp (2.5ml spoon) cumin powder
2 tablesps (2 × 15ml spoons) flour
14oz (400g) can tomatoes
¼ pint (150ml) vegetable stock
6oz (175g) carrots, peeled and sliced
3 sticks celery, sliced
1 aubergine, approximately 10oz (275g), sliced
6oz (175g) cauliflower florets
6oz (175g) courgettes, sliced
salt

1. Heat oil, add nuts, onion, garlic and spices. Fry for 5 minutes, until golden. Add flour and cook for a further 2-3 minutes. Blend in tomatoes with their juice, and stock. Bring to the boil.

2. Add carrot and celery. Cover pan and simmer for 10 minutes.

3. Stir in aubergine, cauliflower and courgette. Season to taste, cover and simmer for a further 25 minutes until vegetables are cooked.

Serves 6

Sweet Chestnut Roulade

A special occasion dessert, substitute 10oz (275g) fresh chestnuts if available – slit the rounded side of the shells and blanch for 5 minutes. Drain and remove shells before simmering nuts for a further 35-40 minutes. The grated chocolate gives this roulade an unusual speckled effect.

Roulade
3 (size 3) eggs, separated
3oz (75g) caster sugar
3oz (75g) dark chocolate, grated
1 tablesp (15ml spoon) boiling water

Filling
4oz (125g) dried chestnuts, soaked overnight in boiling water
4oz (125g) curd cheese
2 tablesps (2 × 15ml spoons) kirsch
1oz (25g) icing sugar
icing sugar for dusting
marron glacés or grated chocolate for decorating

1. Grease and line an 11" × 7" (28cm × 18cm) swiss roll tin.

2. Whisk egg yolks and sugar until light and thick, about 10 minutes.

3. Stiffly beat egg whites. Fold into whisked mixture alternately with grated chocolate. Fold in water and pour into prepared tin. Shake to level surface.

4. Bake at 180°C, 350°F, gas 4 for 20 minutes until set. Cover with a sheet of greaseproof paper and damp teatowel. Leave overnight or for at least 3 hours.

5. Drain chestnuts. Place in a pan of fresh water, bring to the boil, cover and simmer for 45 minutes until tender. Drain and cool.

6. Purée chestnuts. Add cheese, kirsch and icing sugar and blend until smooth.

7. Turn roulade out onto a sheet of greaseproof paper dusted with icing sugar. Spread ¾ chestnut filling over surface and roll up roulade from short edge, swiss roll fashion. Pipe remaining chestnut purée down centre and decorate with marron glacés or grated chocolate. Chill before serving.

Serves 8.

Pecan Apple Shortbread

Serve at tea time or as a dessert with custard or rice pudding.

Filling
1lb (450g) cooking apples, peeled, cored and roughly chopped
3oz (75g) sultanas
2oz (50g) soft light brown sugar
grated rind and juice of 1 orange
½ teasp (2.5ml spoon) cinnamon

Shortbread
12oz (350g) wholemeal flour
4oz (125g) shelled pecan nuts, 12 halves reserved, remainder ground
7oz (200g) polyunsaturated margarine
4oz (125g) soft light brown sugar
1 (size 3) egg yolk

1. Place apples, sultanas, sugar, orange rind and juice and cinnamon in a pan. Simmer, uncovered, for about 10 minutes until the apples are just soft and liquid evaporated. Cool slightly.

2. Mix flour and ground nuts in a bowl. Cream together fat and sugar until light and fluffy. Beat in egg yolk.

3. Fork dry ingredients into creamed mixture. Press half into the base

of an 8″ (20cm) loose bottomed round cake tin. Spread apple mixture over surface.

4. On a lightly floured surface roll out remaining dough to an 8″ (20cm) round and place over filling. Prick surface all over with a fork and arrange reserved pecans around edge.

5. Bake at 180°C, 350°F, gas 4 for about 1¼ hours until golden. Turn out onto a wire rack and divide into 12 wedges before cooling.

Makes 12.

Monkey Buns

A favourite with children, these high fibre buns make teatime special and are also ideal for packed lunches. If easy blend yeast is used ½ sachet will be sufficient. No batter need be set, simply stir in yeast after rubbing fat into flour and salt. Stir in milk, honey and egg and continue as for traditional method.

Batter
2 teasps (2 × 5ml spoons) dried yeast and 1 teasp (5ml spoon) honey,
or ½oz (15g) fresh yeast
3fl oz (75ml) hand hot milk
2oz (50g) strong brown flour

Dough
6oz (175g) strong brown flour
½ teasp (2.5ml spoon) salt
1oz (25g) polyunsaturated margarine
1 tablesp (15ml spoon) honey
1 (size 3) egg, beaten

Filling
4oz (125g) dried dates, chopped
1 tablesp (15ml spoon) lemon juice
1oz (25g) creamed coconut, roughly chopped
2 medium bananas, thinly sliced
1 tablesp (15ml spoon) desiccated coconut

1. Sprinkle dried yeast and honey over milk and leave for 5 minutes. Alternatively dissolve fresh yeast in milk. Stir in flour and allow to stand for 20 minutes until frothy.

2. Rub fat into flour and salt. Stir honey and egg into yeast mixture. Add to dry ingredients and form into a soft dough. Knead for about 10 minutes until smooth. Place in a greased polythene bag and leave in a warm place until doubled in size.

3. Simmer dates in lemon juice for 2-3 minutes until pulpy. Remove from heat and stir in creamed coconut until mixture is smooth. Add banana and allow to cool.

4. Preheat oven 220°C, 425°F, gas 7. Lightly grease a 7″ (18cm) square tin.

5. Roll out dough on a floured surface into a 12″ × 9″ (30cm × 23cm) rectangle. Spread evenly with banana mixture leaving a ½″ (12.5mm) border around edges. Roll up tightly from long edge and divide into 9 rounds. Place in prepared tin and sprinkle with coconut. Cover and leave in a warm place for about 45 minutes until doubled in size.

6. Bake for 20-25 minutes until golden brown. Cool on wire rack.

Makes 9.

Sesame and Oat Nuggets

These wholesome biscuits are delicious as a snack or served with yoghurt or fresh fruit.

4oz (125g) self-raising wholemeal flour
3oz (75g) dried dates, chopped
3oz (75g) rolled oats
1oz (25g) sesame seeds
1oz (25g) custard powder
4oz (125g) polyunsaturated margarine
2oz (50g) soft dark brown sugar
2 tablesps (2 × 15ml spoons) golden syrup
1 (size 3) egg, beaten

1. Combine flour, dates, oats, sesame seeds and custard powder in a bowl.

2. Cream together fat, sugar and syrup until light and fluffy. Gradually beat in egg. Add dry ingredients and mix well.

3. Using floured hands shape walnut-sized pieces of mixture into balls. Place on a greased baking sheet and flatten with a fork.

4. Bake at 180°C, 350°F, gas 4 for 15 minutes, until golden. Cool on a wire rack.

Makes 34-36 biscuits.

CHAPTER 4
Fruits

One of the major benefits of modern transport, storage and packaging advances, in relation to food, is the increasing varieties of exotic fruits which are becoming widely available throughout the year. Their radiant hues of reds, greens, oranges and pinks are full of the warmth of their tropical homelands, bringing colour and interest to today's cooking – and thus opening whole new horizons for experimentation. In addition to the colours, flavours and textures which they add to dishes these fruits are also valuable in the diet as sources of fibre and are rich in vitamins (particularly vitamins A, C and D) and minerals, needed for good health.

It is no mistake that writers have been slow to include these fruits in recipes, since to fully appreciate their fine flavours exotic fruits are most refreshing eaten, as they are by the natives, in their natural state, or confined to being, at most, incorporated with delicate flavourings in ices, creams and fruit salads.

One of the difficulties when choosing unfamiliar fruit is to know what points to look for. As a general guide the fruit is ripe when it "gives" slightly when pressed, but be careful to avoid very soft, over ripe fruit. Under ripe, green fruit will ripen if left in a warm place for 2-3 days. Once matured soft fruits should be eaten at once, since they will only keep for one to two days. Another obstacle in selection is the confusion which may arise in identifying the fruit – descriptions of each are given in this chapter and are often a more reliable guide than the names, which tend to differ according to the country in which the fruit was grown. Italian persimmons are a classic example, since when imported from Israel they are known as Sharon Fruit. Currently many of these unfamiliar fruits are on the expensive side due to the economics of supply and demand, but as popular varieties become established so prices will come down.

There are also now many more varieties of dried fruit on the shelves. These embody all the goodness of fresh fruit but in a concentrated form. High in fibre (figs and apricots in particular), vitamins and minerals, they are naturally sweet and can therefore be added to cereals instead of sprinkling on sugar, and if incorporated into cakes and puddings the amount of sugar used may be reduced. Drying is a major form of preservation, although not so popular now as in the days before freezers arrived. Originally the fruits would be dried in the sun but now this process is mainly carried out under artificial conditions. Kept in a cool, dark place in an airtight container the fruit may be stored for 6-12 months. Mixtures of dried fruits for use in fruit salads/compotes are available, as well as different types being sold separately. Apples, apricots, dates, figs, grapes, peaches, pears and prunes are all readily available in a dried state. Use either as they are or plump up by soaking overnight, or simmering until they swell.

AVOCADO PEAR

Also known as "alligator pear" or "butter fruit", avocado pears are grown in America, Africa and the Far East. Most imports come from Israel and South America, ensuring that avocados are available all year. There are two main varieties – the long, smooth skinned, green, pear-shaped avocados and the rounder, Hass which have knobbly, deep purple skin. In addition cocktail/finger avocados can sometimes be found. These are about the same length as Hass avocados but oblong with a diameter of 1" (2.5cm), and have smooth, green skins. Contrary to the nutrient composition of other fruits avocados are very high in fat, containing about 20% oil. Rich in vitamin A the flesh has a butter-like texture and mild, nutty flavour which is only fully appreciated when the avocado is ripe, that is when the thinner end feels soft when gently pressed. To prepare; score skin into quarters and peel back with a knife. Halve fruit lengthways, twist to separate pieces and remove stone. Sprinkle with lemon juice to prevent browning. Avocados are usually served as a starter with sweet or savoury ingredients – orange or prawns are favourite fillings – tossed in a little dressing. Finger avocados can be sliced into salads or puréed. They make a delicious dip, served in Mexico as guacamole which combines garlic, tomato and chilli powder with puréed avocado.

CAPE GOOSEBERRY, PHYSALIS, TIPPARI or PERUVIAN CHERRY

Peruvian in origin, the Cape gooseberry is also cultivated in the tropics, Ceylon, India, Mexico and is commonly found in Africa – particularly in the Cape of the South, hence the derivation of its English name. These intriguing fruits are the size of small cherries encased by pale green, ripening to beige, parchment-like bracts. They are better known as Chinese lanterns. The edible fruit turn from green through to orange on maturing, and the shrub can be harvested just three months from planting. To prepare; remove brittle casing, rinse and dry fruit. Use whole, or halve to reveal the mass of tiny seeds. Cape gooseberries have a sharp, berry-like flavour and may be eaten raw in salads, poached or puréed with other fruit or blended with custard to make a fruit fool. For use as an unusual decoration, simply peel back papery husk from pointed end to reveal fruit. Store at room temperature and eat at once when ripe.

CARAMBOLA or STAR FRUIT

"Star fruit" is another name for carambola since the five longitudinal ribs which run down the length of the fruit give the effect of a star when the fruit is sliced across its width. Indigenous to Malaysia and Indonesia carambolas are available throughout South East Asia and are now grown in many tropical countries as well as parts of America. Imports come from Brazil and Israel. This five sided, oblong, tropical fruit has yellow waxy skin (green when unripe), measures 5"-6" (12.5cm-15cm) in length and grows on a tree which flowers and bears fruit simultaneously. Available intermittently throughout the year the fruits are thin skinned and contain up to 12 flat seeds which are removed as from lemon slices. The crisp, translucent flesh has a refreshing lemony/pineapple flavour. Rich in vitamin C carambolas are easily prepared; wipe and peel away any black lines down the ridges, slice off ends and cut across to produce star-shaped slices which look very attractive floated in drinks. Carambolas keep well, stored in a cool place, and impart a delicious flavour to fruit salads and jellies, their sharpness balancing well with the sweetness of other fruit. They may also be stewed or used in preserves, and are traditionally cooked with chicken in Asia.

Carrambola (Star Fruit)

CITRUS FRUIT

Kumquat – although not strictly a citrus fruit, kumquats, or "dwarf oranges" as they are sometimes called, follow the characteristics of this family. They resemble an elongated, date sized orange (although some varieties are more rounded) with thick, edible skin. The acidic flesh contains a few pips. Native to the Far East, *kumquats are now cultivated in many countries with a hot climate – main imports come from Brazil. Fresh kumquats are available all year and may also be bought preserved in liqueur. Wash and dry before slicing into rings. Their bitter/sweet taste is ideal for preserves, or as an accompaniment to meat. Green patches, sometimes present on the skin, will ripen naturally in the sun.

Minneola – a cross between an orange, tangerine and grapefruit, minneolas are apple-sized, with a shiny, deep orange skin, and characterised by a distinctive nipple at the base. Available from January – May, the flesh of minneolas is tender and very juicy, with a strong tangerine/orange flavour. They are high in vitamin C and can be prepared and used in the same way as oranges.

Orantique – imported from the West Indies orantiques are the size of oranges, but tangerine shaped with very thin, pale yellow-orange skin and large, fleshy segments. A cross between an orange and tangerine the flesh is very juicy and sweet. Orantiques are a good source of vitamin C, and carotene, and available from December to June for use in preserves and desserts.

Pomelo

Pomelo – "shaddock" or "forbidden fruit" are alternative names for the pomelo. These enormous yellow-green skinned citrus fruit are pear-shaped and have very thick pith and pale flesh. Popular in the Far East, imports come from Israel. Pomelos have a similar taste to grapefruit, but are less sharp and have a coarser flesh. Peel as for oranges and use the thick skin for marmalade making and the flesh in cooking as a substitute for grapefruit.

*Their name is taken from the Cantonese word kam quat, meaning "gold orange".

Ugli – also known as "tangelo", uglies are so called because of their irregular, bumpy appearance. A cross between a grapefruit and tangerine, uglies have green-yellow skin and juicy, sweet, orange flesh, with a few pips. 4"-6" (10cm-15cm) in diameter they are native to Jamaica and available from January through to June. Eat as an orange (uglies are sweet enough not to need added sugar) or chop the large segments and mix with avocado and watercress for a light, refreshing salad.

CRANBERRY or BOUNCEBERRY

Introduced to the Pilgrim settlers in North America by the Red Indians, cranberries grow wild in peat bogs, although under cultivation, conditions are simulated and the land is smothered with sea sand and then flooded to provide ideal conditions for the plant's growth. The name cranberry resulted from the shape of the plant's pink flowers which resemble a crane's head, hence the plant was originally termed "Craneberry". Cranberry plants blossom in late June – early July, and are harvested in September, through the Autumn. Imports of fresh cranberries reach this country for October and are available through January, although bottled sauces and jellies can be purchased all year round. Initially pale yellow the large oval/round, shiny berries ripen to a deep red colour. Their sharp flavour necessitates cooking – simmer until the skins just burst, since overcooking to a slush tends to increase their bitterness. Fresh cranberries freeze well for use throughout the year in preserves, sauces, stuffings, cakes, pies, punches, or a delicious sweet-sour glaze for poultry, lamb and pork. For an unusual winter flan simmer cranberries in orange juice with a little sugar and cinnamon, and use as a pastry or sponge flan filling.

CUSTARD APPLE or ANNONA FRUIT

These are grown in many tropical countries and very popular in the West Indies and South America. Almost round in shape the green-purple-yellow-brown skin encloses creamy white, smooth pulp which contains up to eighty black, inedible seeds. Ripe custard apples are juicy, have a sweet/sour taste and contain vitamin C and minerals, particularly calcium. Peel and discard seeds before eating raw or adding to milk based puddings, fruit salads or puréeing for a sauce. Custard apples are best stored at room temperature as they do not keep well under refrigeration.

61

FEIJOA or PINEAPPLE GUAVA

The fruit of a Brazilian tree, now also grown in Asia, Africa and New Zealand (where most imports come from), feijoas are available from May to October and have thin, smooth, bottle green-grey skins. Approximating in size and shape to a large egg this fruit has yellow, granular flesh which surrounds a red jellied pulp in which the edible black seeds are housed. Rich in vitamins the flavour of feijoas lies somewhere between that of pineapple, strawberries and guavas, hence its alternative name "pineapple guava". In fact it is a close relative to the guava and can be used in the same ways; peel and add raw to fruit salads, poach and purée or use as a pie filling. Once ripe, that is when slightly soft to the touch, feijoas should be eaten as soon as possible.

GUAVA

Native to India, guavas are now widely grown in Brazil, South America, Mexico, California and the West Indies. This tropical fruit is available all year round although spring-summer is the peak season. The most common variety in this country is the South African guava which has a green skin, ripening to yellow. Brazilian guavas are purple skinned with salmon pink flesh and mainly found in a canned form. Both have a strong, distinctive, musky aroma. To test for ripeness the fruit should yield when lightly pressed. Peel guavas and scoop out the hard seeds in the centre of the milky flesh before using raw in ices, mousses and yoghurt or adding to desserts, jams, jellies or cheesecakes. Guavas are an excellent source of vitamin C, containing up to five times as much as citrus fruit. They also contain vitamin A, calcium and iron as well as being a good source of dietary fibre. When cooked guavas hold their shape well and are therefore well suited to use in pies and crumbles.

KIWI FRUIT or CHINESE GOOSEBERRY

Grown in China since ancient times kiwis are consequently also referred to as "Chinese gooseberries". Only since the beginning of this century have they been cultivated in New Zealand where they were renamed "kiwi" due to the resemblance of their shape and magical colours to the wingless national bird. Kenya, Italy, America and France also grow kiwi fruit which are available throughout the year. Their shape varies from an elongated oval to a rounder, egg-sized fruit. The soft, furry, brown-grey coloured, inedible skin is peeled to reveal bright green flesh, which has a surprisingly subtle flavour, and is studded with deep purple seeds which surround a soft, pale green central core. To test for ripeness the fruit should give slightly to the touch but not feel very soft. Unripe kiwis ripen in a couple of days under warm conditions. Kiwis are very rich in vitamin C as well as containing appreciable amounts of vitamins A and D, iron, calcium and a protein dissolving enzyme which makes them an effective meat tenderiser. Their mild flavour favours use in both sweet and savoury dishes. The fruit is also very attractive as a decoration – sliced, diced or cut into wedges.

Kiwi Fruit

LONGAN

Originally from India longans subsequently spread to China and a number of tropical countries. A relation of the lychee and rambutan, they resemble the former in appearance – being slightly more rounded, with a duller brown bark. Longans are often sold with pieces of their brittle branch still attached. Their creamy semi-translucent flesh encloses a shiny, dark brown, inedible stone. To test for ripeness the flesh should pop out when the bark is pierced. Choose even sized, plump looking fruit which have not already split. Longans have a sweet, grape-like flavour and are slightly more aromatic than lychees. They also respond well to canning and are available during the summer.

LOQUAT, JAPANESE MEDLAR or JAPANESE PLUM

Native to China the fruit then spread to Japan and is now cultivated in India, Africa, part of the Mediterranean and Australia. Similar to a large apricot in shape and colour, having the characteristic downy skin and firm, sweet, yellow-orange flesh. Instead of one central stone, they may contain up to five, grouped in a cluster in the middle and surrounded with a fibrous film. Since the skin is slightly tough it is often peeled away. Halve and remove the inedible, smooth, shiny brown stones (which can be added to the pan when poaching the fruit to give an almondy flavour). Loquats are also delicious raw in fruit salads or combined with summer fruit, since they are available during spring and summer, in a liqueur.

LYCHEE

Also spelt "litchi", these were originally grown in the Far East where they are still widely used. Primarily a Chinese fruit lychees are now grown in India, Australia, South Africa, Kenya, Brazil and Israel. The size of a strawberry, lychees have thin, brittle, bark-like skins which are multi-coloured; purple- pink-brown. Peel to reveal pearly white, juicy flesh, similar in texture to grapes, with a distinctive fragrant, sweet taste. The soft flesh encases a hard, shiny, dark brown stone which must be removed before serving. Fruit picked under ripe will not mature fully so ensure that the fruit is firm and plump and the skins bright and unbroken. Fresh lychees are available all year round, being most plentiful in the winter and spring, and can be frozen whole, unskinned, for 3 months. The juice from canned lychees should not be wasted as it makes a delicious sorbet. Lychees are an excellent source of vitamin C, fresh more so than canned, and combine well with strawberries and liqueur or may be puréed and added to ices, yoghurt desserts and cheesecakes. Store for 1-2 weeks at room temperature.

Lychees

MANGO

A popular tropical fruit of South East Asian origin, known to be at least 4,000 years old, mangoes are also grown in Africa, the Philippines, California and Mexico, with main imports coming from Kenya and Brazil. The Brazilian variety tends to be rounder than the more oval, kidney-shaped strain which have pointed ends. Abroad sizes can vary between that of an orange, up to a weight of 5lbs (2.2kg). The skin turns from green to yellow, through orange to red as it ripens, and should feel tender. Unripe mangoes have a "turpentine-like" flavour. Ideally they should have a sweet fragrance and distinctive taste. Available throughout the year mangoes are made up of 10-20% sugars and are a good source of vitamin A and C. The large flat stones cling to the flesh making them somewhat difficult to remove. The easiest way is, once the mango is peeled, to horizontally cut a slice off each side, keeping the blade of the knife as near to the stone as possible, and then cut away the remaining flesh. The juicy orange flesh is delicious on its own, served chilled, or used to flavour mousses, creams, jellies and cheesecakes. Green mangoes are excellent in pickles and chutneys. Canned mangoes, already prepared, are also available.

MANGOSTEEN

Mainly cultivated in the hot, humid climate of South East Asia, although now also grown in South America, mangosteens are expensive because they are difficult to grow; once successfully planted the tree takes 15-20 years before it bears fruit, which makes large scale production uneconomical. The tomato-sized, round berries have a smooth, hard skin, are dark purple in colour with the flower petals still surrounding the stalk in a ruff even after ripening. To prepare; remove top half of the shell with a knife and prise away the flesh. Mangosteens keep well but once exposed to the atmosphere they brown and should therefore be eaten at once. The flesh is similar in appearance to lychees, but divided into four or more plump segments which contain inedible green seeds. Traditionally the white juicy flesh is eaten raw because of its prized delicate flavour. Alternatively purée for use in ices. Mangosteens are available at spasmodic intervals between spring and autumn.

PAPAYA or PAW PAW

This fruit is known in areas of cultivation as "the fruit of the medicine tree" because of its multi-remedy properties. The seeds are often chewed to aid digestion and although edible are usually discarded in this country. The enzyme papain, responsible for the digestion of proteins, is present in unripe fruits – papain based tablets are sold to relieve indigestion and by cooking the fruit with meat a tender result is achieved – although ripe papaya contain a lesser amount. This enzyme also has a weakening effect on gelatine when used in conjunction with it in recipes – such as for soufflés and mousses. Grown throughout the tropics, although originally from Central America, the large, pear-shaped fruit have a delicious, unique flavour. Papayas bought in this country weigh about 8oz (225g) although those grown in the tropics can be as much as 20lb (9kg). From green the skins ripen to yellow and the flesh a vivid orange-pink. Yet another name for this fruit is "melon of the tropics" or "tree melon", because of its similar, although denser texture to melon. Inside the cavity is filled with a mass of grey-black "peppercorn-like" seeds. The fruits bruise easily and are ripe when just soft. Peel the thin skin, halve, remove seeds and serve sprinkled with lime juice, chop and add to salads, or purée for ices and milk shakes. See page no. 113/114 for cheesecake recipe. Green papaya, found in West Indian shops are eaten as a vegetable and are delicious in pickles and chutneys. Nutritionally ripe papayas contain appreciable amounts of vitamins A and C.

PASSION FRUIT

Three strains of this fruit are imported into this country – the popular purple-brown, wrinkled variety, lined with a thick, pinky, rubbery layer which encloses the orange, jelly-like pulp surrounding the crunchy purple seeds which are edible. This tropical vine fruit comes from South Brazil but also grows in Mediterranean and tropical climates as well as in New Zealand. Available all year round this is the most common variety. Do not be afraid to choose wizened looking fruit since this is a sign of ripeness. A similar variety, but yellow in appearance, comes from the tropics. Slightly larger than the purple passion fruit it is also wrinkly but has a more acidic taste and less pulp. More unusual is the sweet grenadilla which is about three times the size of other passion fruit, round in shape with smooth orange skin dappled with red, rather like a pomegranate. A ½″ (12.5mm) thick, polystyrene-like case encloses the yellowy pulp and greyish seeds which are not as sweet as those in the purple variety. To prepare; using a sharp knife halve the fruit and scoop out seeds. Passion fruit have an exquisitely pungent, tropical flavour which combines well with other fruits in yoghurt desserts, ices, crumbles and drinks. Chilling helps bring out their flavour. See page 114 for "Passion Peach Mousse".

PERSIMMON or SHARON FRUIT

Having originated in the Far East (Japan and China) this fruit is now widely cultivated in Southern France, Israel, Italy, South America, California, Florida, India and Australia. The variety imported from Israel is sold as "Sharon Fruit", whilst "Persimmons" come from Italy. Persimmons are similar in appearance to large orange tomatoes with shiny, smooth skins and dark green, ruff-like leaves. The pulpy, orange, seedless flesh is rich in vitamin A. Since persimmons have a high acid content, unless the fruit is fully ripe when eaten – that is feels slightly tender to the touch and may sometimes be spotted with brown sugar patches – it will have a rough, starchy taste. Preparation is minimal; remove stalk, wash and dry fruit and slice as required. The thin skin is edible and persimmons are delicious raw or cooked. Purée for fools, jellies and ices. An excellent sauce to accompany sorbets, ice creams or pancakes can be made by puréeing the fruit with lime juice and sweetening if necessary with icing sugar. Persimmons are scarce during the summer months.

POMEGRANATE

Grown in the Mediterranean, Middle East, California, South America and The Canary Islands most imports come from Spain. On average, pomegranates are the size of an orange, their thin, smooth, leathery skin varying in colour between pink, beige and yellow. The fruit is distinguished by its calyx. To prepare; peel away skin and the bitter pale yellow membrane which divides the clusters of translucent crimson flesh surrounding the long white seeds. Pomegranates have an unique taste and their juicy, crisp flesh is usually eaten raw, or used for jellies. The juice is the source of grenadine syrup and can also be used in fruit salads and sorbets. Pomegranates are available from August to January.

PRICKLY PEAR, INDIAN FIG or CACTUS FRUIT

Prickly Pear

Native to the American desert where the fruit grows on cactus, prickly pears are now cultivated in tropical and Mediterranean climates as well as in Australia. They are picked whilst still green and left to ripen until blushed with orange and pink. More potato-shaped than pear, small thickenings on the skin house clusters of prickles, so care is therefore needed when peeling. The easiest way being to steady the pear with a fork, slice off each end, make a lengthwise slit and pare away skin to reveal flesh. Orange in colour the flesh is embedded with small, crunchy brown seeds which are edible. Available during late summer and the winter months choose firm, well coloured fruit, free from blemishes and keep refrigerated for up to two weeks. Prickly pears have a sweet flavour, somewhere between that of pear and melon, which contrasts well with the acidic sharpness of lemon. Slice into fruit salads, combine with thick yoghurt for a coffee gâteau or meringue filling or use in crumbles.

RAMBUTAN

Of Malaysian origin, predominantly grown in South East Asia, rambutans look more like colourful, hairy creatures than a fruit! Their oval shape is masked by long, curly, soft spines of varigating colour, turning from green through to crimson-brown on ripening. The thin, tough casing encloses a white, translucent, juicy flesh, similar to its relation – the lychee. To prepare; break off stem, make a slit in the skin and squeeze out flesh and juice. Pare light brown central seed from flesh and eat raw or cooked in fruit compotes, ices, flans or gateaux. Rambutans have a refreshing sweet-sour flavour and are a good source of vitamin C. Their high price is due to the fruit's limited cultivation and perishable nature.

Rambutan

SAPODILLA or MARMALADE PLUM

Originally cultivated in Central America this fruit is now widely grown throughout the tropics. Many varieties exist although the sapodillas imported into this country are similar to hairless kiwi fruit. To prepare; peel tough skin (if it comes away easily then the fruit is ripe), remove the few long, hard, hooked, black seeds and chop the salmon pink flesh. Sapodillas have a rubbery texture which is also slightly granular in a similar way to quinces. Their stringent flavour, hence their alternative name, necessitates sweetening. Use in pies and crumbles, poach, or add to fruit salads. Sapodillas are a good source of calcium. Supplies come from Thailand during November-May. Choose those which yield slightly to the touch, since unripe fruits have a very sharp taste, and store at room temperature. The milky fluid derived from the sapodilla plant is used in the manufacture of chewing gum.

68

TAMARILLO, JAVA PLUM, TREE TOMATO or JAMBOLA

Native to Peru this shrub has long been cultivated in South America and over the centuries spread to East Africa, South East Asia, New Zealand and Australia. A member of the nightshade family, the egg-shaped fruit has smooth, yellow-scarlet skin, streaked with crimson. In appearance it resembles a Victoria plum which, coupled with its likeness in colour and texture to a tomato, earns it two of the alternative names. Available from April to September, tamarillos have a sharp, acidic, tropical flavour, faintly resembling apricots/tomatoes. Contained in the orange flesh are many dark red, crunchy seeds. The fruit is rich in vitamins, particularly A and C, as well as the mineral, iron. Choose those which feel tender to the touch and peel (the skin has a bitter taste) before eating raw or cooked. Tamarillos also add a lovely colour to preserves. Wrap in a plastic bag and refrigerate for up to 2 weeks.

TAMARIND or DATE OF INDIA

Native to the West Indies and the tropics of Africa where the tamarind tree grows wild, thriving on poor soils, cultivated forms are grown in Western Asia and India. The semi-evergreen tree fruits after 7-8 years to produce 6"-8" (15cm-20cm) long legumes (through which the seeds can be traced), with cocoa coloured, brittle shells, enclosing a sticky, brown fibrous pulp which contains the glossy, hard black seeds. The tree serves many purposes for the local natives – the leaves and flowers being used as a vegetable in salads and curries, flour is ground from the cooked beans and the tree timber used for charcoal or reserved for carpentry. Tamarinds are a mild laxative, contain about 10% tartaric acid and are naturally high in sugars, which accounts for their sweet-sour taste, reminiscent of gooseberries and cherries. The edible pulp is not easily separated from the beans and must either be covered with boiling water and left to soak overnight or boiled for 10 minutes, before pushing through a sieve to obtain a purée. Tamarinds are also called "Dates of India" because of the date-like appearance and texture of the pulp which can consequently be used as a substitute. It is also widely included in curry dishes as a flavouring. Tamarinds are a good source of B vitamins, especially niacin, calcium and iron. Available fresh, in blocks containing the pulp and seed, or as a refined extract, when buying fresh tamarinds look for brittle pods – since this is a sign of ripeness – and choose those which have not been broken.

TOMATOES

Technically a fruit, tomatoes are often thought of as a vegetable because of the ingredients with which they are combined. In addition to the round tomatoes, commonly grown in this country, other varieties are becoming increasingly popular. These include-

Beef tomatoes – also known as "Mediterranean tomatoes" since they are widely used in the cooking of this region. These large, flattened, deeply ridged tomatoes have very thick flesh. Ideal for stuffing they do not have as much flavour as the round tomatoes but can be eaten raw, combining well with slices of Mozarella cheese and a chive vinaigrette.

Cherry tomatoes – small, round, approximately the size of a two pence coin in diameter, these tomatoes are usually served whole and are ideal for salads or garnishes.

Choose firm, bright, red fruits with fresh looking green stalks. Tomatoes are rich in vitamins A and C as well as containing some trace minerals. Imports ensure that supplies are available nearly all year round, although summer is the most plentiful time for homegrown cherry tomatoes.

Pork with Kumquat Sauce

Kumquats and marmalade give the pork a delightful bitter-sweet flavour. Serve with a leafy green vegetable and jacket potatoes.

2 tablesps (2 × 15ml spoons) oil
1½lbs (700g) lean pork, cubed
1 large onion
2 tablesps (2 × 15ml spoons) flour
½ pint (300ml) stock
4 tablesps (4 × 15ml spoons) no added sugar marmalade
½lb (225g) kumquats, washed and sliced
salt and pepper

70

1. Heat oil. Add pork and cook until brown. Drain meat and set aside.

2. Add onion to pan and brown. Stir in flour and cook until golden.

3. Blend in stock and marmalade and bring to the boil. Return meat to pan, add kumquats and season to taste.

4. Cover and simmer over a low heat for 30 minutes until pork is tender.

Serves 4.

Sunset Pancakes

Serve these fruity pancakes with natural yoghurt or smetana. The reserved fruit juice makes a refreshing drink. If you prefer to use wholemeal flour, then self-raising will give a lighter result.

Pancake batter
3oz (75g) plain flour
1 teasp (5ml spoon) cinnamon
1 (size 3) egg
7fl oz (200ml) skimmed milk
oil

Filling
2 × 300g cans raspberries in fruit juice, drained
2 teasps (2 × 5ml spoons) sugar
20 cape gooseberries
2 teasps (2 × 5ml spoons) kirsch

1. Mix flour and cinnamon in a bowl. Add egg and half milk, beat to a smooth batter. Gradually whisk in remaining milk.

2. Heat a little oil in a 7" (18cm) diameter omelette pan. Pour off any excess. Spoon enough batter to just cover base into pan and cook for 1-2 minutes until set. Flip pancake over and cook until golden. Use batter to make 6 pancakes. Keep warm in a low oven.

3. Sieve ¾ raspberries and place in a pan with sugar. Break open cape gooseberries and twist out berry. Wash, dry and halve.

4. Dissolve sugar in raspberry purée over a gentle heat. Add cape gooseberries to pan and poach for 1-2 minutes until just soft. Remove from heat and stir in kirsch and reserved whole raspberries.

5. Fold pancakes in half, and then half again. Spoon a little filling into each and pour remaining sauce over top. Serve at once.

Serves 6.

Star Fruit Compote

Ideally the fruits should be allowed to "mature" for 24 hours so that they plump up and take on the flavours of the various spices.

½ pint (300ml) white grape juice
2 teasps (2 × 5ml spoons) brown sugar
1 stick cinnamon bark
seeds of 3 green cardamon pods, crushed
4 carambola, sliced
3oz (75g) dried apricots
3oz (75g) prunes
1oz (25g) sultanas

1. Stir grape juice, sugar, cinnamon stick and cardamon over a gentle heat until sugar dissolves. Bring to the boil, cover and simmer for 5 minutes.

2. Pour liquor over fruit and leave to stand overnight. Stir occasionally. Remove cinnamon bark and serve with thick Greek yoghurt.

Serves 4.

Guava and Apricot Ice

Guava and apricot blend perfectly to give a deliciously smooth ice.

2 (size 3) eggs, separated
2oz (50g) soft brown sugar
2 guavas, peeled, deseeded and roughly chopped
14½oz (411g) can apricot halves in natural juice, drained
or 8 fresh apricots, stoned and roughly chopped
2 teasps (2 × 5ml spoons) lemon juice
5.29oz (150g) carton natural low fat yoghurt
5fl oz (142ml) carton ½ fat double cream

1. Whisk egg yolks and sugar until thick and creamy.

2. Purée guavas, apricots and lemon juice in a liquidiser/processor until smooth. Fold into egg mixture.

3. Place yoghurt and cream in a bowl and whisk until thick. Fold into egg mixture and pour into a rigid container. Freeze until just beginning to set.

4. Stiffly whisk whites. Beat cream mixture until smooth, to break up ice crystals. Carefully fold in whites. Cover and return to freezer until solid. Remove 10 minutes before serving to allow to soften slightly.

Serves 6-8.

White Mountain Fruit Gâteau

An impressive, colourful gâteau for special occasions which is not too sweet.

Sponge
2½oz (65g) plain flour
½oz (15g) custard powder
3 (size 3) eggs, separated
3oz (75g) caster sugar

Filling
2 tablesps (2 × 15ml spoons) cointreau
5.29oz (150g) carton natural low fat yoghurt
5fl oz (142ml) carton whipping cream
12 lychees, peeled, stoned and halved
2 kiwi fruit, peeled and thinly sliced
4oz (125g) strawberries, hulled and quartered

1. Sift flour and custard powder 2-3 times until thoroughly mixed.

2. Place eggs and sugar in a large bowl and, using an electric whisk, beat for 10 minutes until thick and creamy and beaters leave a trail.

3. Gradually fold in flour mixture. Pour into a greased and lined 7" (18cm) round cake tin. Shake gently to level surface and bake at 180°C, 350°F, gas 4 for 30-35 minutes until risen and golden. Turn out onto a wire rack, remove paper and leave to cool.

4. Cut sponge horizontally into 3 and sprinkle 1/3 of the cointreau evenly over each layer.

5. Whisk together yoghurt and cream until mixture forms soft peaks. Reserve 2/3 and use remainder, with 2/3 of prepared fruit, to sandwich sponge layers together.

6. Spread reserved yoghurt mixture over top and side of gâteau and pile fruit on top. Chill for a couple of hours before serving to allow flavours to mingle.

Serves 12.

Mango Cream

In this low fat dessert mango's distinctive aroma and flavour blends with cardamon conjuring up a taste of India.

¼ pint (150ml) orange juice
seeds of 4 cardamon pods
1 mango, approx. weight 12oz (350g)
4oz (125g) half fat cottage cheese
1 (size 3) egg white
1 tablesp (15ml spoon) caster sugar

1. Place orange juice and cardamon seeds in a small pan. Cover and bring slowly to the boil. Remove from heat and leave to infuse until cool. Strain and reserve juice.

2. Peel mango, cut flesh from stone and place in a liquidiser/processor. Purée to a pulp. Add cottage cheese and continue processing until smooth. Gradually pour in strained juice until thoroughly blended.

3. Whisk egg white to a soft peak. Add sugar and continue beating until stiff.

4. Fold into mango mixture, pour into serving dish and chill.

Serves 4-6.

Scarlet Crumble

Tamarillos conjure up the flavour and colours of the tropics, and combine with muesli to make a wholesome pudding. Serve with natural yoghurt.

4 tamarillos
2 teasps (2 × 5ml spoons) soft brown sugar
good pinch of cinnamon
2 tablesps (2 × 15ml spoons) orange juice

Topping
2oz (50g) unsweetened muesli
2oz (50g) plain wholemeal flour
2oz (50g) polyunsaturated margarine
1 tablesp (15ml spoon) soft brown sugar

1. Peel and roughly dice tamarillos. Place in a ¾ pint (450ml) oval ovenproof dish. Sprinkle with sugar, cinnamon and orange juice.

2. Rub fat into muesli and flour. Stir in sugar and sprinkle over fruit. Press down lightly.

3. Bake at 200°C, 400°F, gas 6 for 25 minutes until golden.

Serves 4.

Tamarind and Banana Squares

Tamarind gives this recipe a mysterious, unidentifiable flavour. 4oz (125g) chopped dried dates could be substituted if tamarinds are unavailable. An alternative way of preparing the tamarinds is to pour boiling water onto the unshelled pods and leave them to stand overnight before shelling and sieving.

8oz (225g) self-raising brown flour
2oz (50g) rolled oats
½ teasp (2.5ml spoon) cinnamon
4oz (125g) polyunsaturated margarine
4 tablesps (4 × 15ml spoons) golden syrup

Filling
4oz (125g) tamarind pods
2 small ripe bananas

1. Combine flour, oats and cinnamon in a bowl.

2. Warm together fat and syrup until just melted. Pour onto dry ingredients and mix well.

3. Shell tamarinds. Boil for 10 minutes until soft and sieve to separate pulp from seeds. Mash bananas and mix with tamarind paste.

4. Press ⅔ oat mixture into a 7" (18cm) shallow square tin. Spread filling over surface and crumble remaining mixture over top. Press down lightly.

5. Bake at 190°C, 375°F, gas 5 for 25-30 minutes until golden. Leave in tin until cold. Cut into squares.

Makes 9.

CHAPTER 5

━━━━━ Vegetables ━━━━━

The shelves of specialist greengrocers, ethnic stores and the larger supermarkets today brim with a range of unfamiliar vegetables, gathered from all corners of the earth. It is a tribute to modern technology – farming, storage and transport techniques, that such fresh vegetables can be made available to the consumer. Indeed, modern production methods have selected the most favourable characteristics of vegetables and bred higher quality, disease resistant plants from them which consequently result in increased yields. In addition, many vegetables now have extended seasons with the advantage of being available in their fresh state for most of the year.

The flavour of vegetables is undoubtedly best when they are in season and most plentiful. However, in contradiction to other foods, they are also at their least expensive at this time. Most of the exotic vegetables are not yet available frozen, although a few are preserved by canning or drying. Home freezing can be successfully carried out for many vegetables providing they are blanched and immediately plunged into cold water to prevent further cooking. Use only fresh produce and freeze for up to 6 months.

Vegetables contain between 80-95% water, are very low in fat, contain some protein and a valuable amount of dietary fibre. Basically a carbohydrate food they are rich in vitamins and minerals and much prized in the current dietary climate. They also add bulk to the diet whilst contributing only a few calories and therefore are ideal for slimmers. As a rough guide leafy green vegetables contribute carotene (which is converted in the body to vitamin A), vitamin C, calcium, iron and other minerals. Roots provide protein, minerals and vitamins whilst peas and beans are a good source of B vitamins and protein. However, the quantity of nutrients in all vegetables is never static since amounts vary with climate, soil, handling and storage conditions. It is therefore important to buy vegetables in peak condition. Points to look for when buying are covered in this chapter, but preparation techniques in the home are also important to ensure that as few of the vitamins as possible are lost. Vitamin C begins to deteriorate once the vegetable is cut, and, along with the B vitamins, is water-soluble and destroyed by heat. Consequently to benefit most from the vitamins in vegetables it is best to eat them raw in salads or cook for just a short period of time.

The variety of vegetables available is continuously escalating. Their colour and range of textures makes them worthy of higher estimation than they receive at present and provides sound reason for their incorporation as an integral part of recipes rather than just as a side dish.

GLOBE ARTICHOKE

Native to Asia globe artichokes are now widely grown in Italy, France and Israel (the three main exporters), as well as in Egypt, Morocco, Algeria and Spain. A member of the thistle family the bulbs look like rounded pine cones mounted on stalks. The shape of the head varies from round to oval depending on the variety. Nutritionally they are a good source of calcium, potassium and carotene, although not much of the vegetable is edible. Globe artichokes are available almost all year, look for heads which are compact and weighty for their size, and ensure that the leaves show no signs of browning. Store in a cool, dry, dark place for up to a week. For preparation technique see following recipe. Artichokes may be stuffed and baked after boiling or served with a sauce, the fleshy leaves being used as an edible spoon. Usually they are presented as a starter and are equally delicious cold, filled with garlic prawns and parsley in a vinaigrette. Canned artichoke bases, sometimes sold as "fonds", and artichoke hearts are becoming more readily available from supermarkets and delicatessens and are excellent combined in salads or stir-fries, the fonds can be stuffed.

JERUSALEM ARTICHOKE

Jerusalem artichokes originated in Brazil but are now grown in South America and throughout Europe. They are not in fact, as their name implies, related to the globe artichoke at all. Jerusalem is believed to be a corruption of the word "girasole", which is Italian for sunflower, to which this vegetable is related. Yellow, white, purple and red varieties exist although yellow are most prevalent in this country. The artichokes are reminiscent of golden nuggets. They contribute calcium and phosphorus to the diet and are available during the winter months. Choose firm, fresh looking samples which are relatively free from soil. If possible avoid the knobbly ones which prove wasteful on peeling. Only buy as many as are needed at one time since artichokes do not keep well, and store in a cool, dark, dry place. Prepare in the same way as potatoes – either scrub or peel and slice as required. Once cut drop into acidulated water to prevent browning, bring to the boil, cover and simmer for 20-30 minutes. Jerusalem artichokes have a crisp texture and sweetish flavour. Always served cooked, they are superb coated in a cheese sauce and topped with breadcrumbs, or alternatively as a warming soup.

BAMBOO SHOOTS

Asian in origin bamboo shoots are the central shoot of tropical bamboo plants. Available canned in brine this yellow, fibrous vegetable may be purchased in lengths or slices and needs no further cooking. Although of insignificant nutritional value – contributing only a few vitamins and a little protein, they add interest to stir-fried dishes, salads and side dishes. Their flavour benefits from the addition of spicy ingredients – cook with pepper, pineapple and five star spice as an accompaniment to pork.

BREADFRUIT

The doomed cargo of Captain Bligh's ill fated voyage on "The Bounty", breadfruit trees were a precious form of cheap food for slaves in the tropics. The melon-sized fruit, native to the tropics of Asia and the South Sea Islands are imported into this country from the West Indies. Breadfruits have thick, rough, waxy green-yellow, ripening to brown, skin and creamy, starchy flesh with a large inedible central core bearing the seeds. Roasted or boiled, their taste is similar to bread, and their nutritional value akin to that of wheat flour. Bake whole, or slice and boil or fry. Breadfruit is served as a substitute for potato. It does not keep well and is consequently rarely found in this country.

BRINJAL or WHITE EGGPLANT

These are small white aubergines. In an uncultivated form the first aubergines grown in the East Indies were the size and shape of an egg, hence their alternative name of "eggplant". They then spread to China and are now widely used in Mediterranean countries. Brinjals are imported into this country from South Africa. Purple, white and green varieties of aubergines exist, purple being the most commonly available. Brinjals weigh about 4oz (125g) each and should be shiny, firm, unwrinkled and free from blemishes. Store in a cool, dark place for 3-4 days. They contain useful amounts of fibre, potassium and some calcium. On cooking the flesh turns a green-grey colour and the seeds blacken. Wipe and simmer whole for 15-20 minutes, scoop out flesh, chop and add to stuffing ingredients. Alternatively marinade and serve sliced in a salad with chick peas, tomato and freshly chopped basil. Parboiled slices of brinjal may be coated in egg and breadcrumbs, fried and served with a spicy tomato sauce as an appetiser.

CARDOON

This vegetable has no great history having only been used in Southern Europe since the sixteenth century. The Italians are particularly partial to this winter vegetable and only rarely is it found in this country. Cardoons resemble celery, having crisp, white, fleshy, ribbed stalks and large green-grey leaves. Their flavour is akin to globe artichokes, to which they are related. Only the stalks are eaten and these should be simmered for 15-20 minutes. Serve as a side vegetable, poached in red wine for special occasions.

CASSAVA, MANIOC or YUCA

Cassava

Also known as "manioc" or "yuca" and originally from Brazil, this starchy tuber forms the basis of tapioca. Cassava is commonly found in tropical countries and is especially popular in Africa and Asia. A relatively thin, irregular root with bark-like skin and protruding shoots, cassava is high in carbohydrates and contributes calcium and potassium to the diet. Basically there are two main types – bitter and sweet. The former can only be used after cooking since it is poisonous otherwise: it is fermented, pressed (at which stage it can be processed into tapioca flakes or pearls) and dried to produce flour. The sweet variety is peeled, baked whole or sliced, and served in the same way as potato. Look for even sized produce which are fairly clean.

CELERIAC

A Mediterranean vegetable which is now grown in many European countries, most imports come from Israel. Similar in shape to irregular swedes, and correspondingly varying in size, celeriac's knobbly skin must be thickly peeled. Choose the smoothest roots to avoid waste and check that they are heavy for their size. Pale green-fawn in colour, celeriac is available throughout the year. A good source of minerals and fibre its flavour is similar to that of celery, to which it is related. Stored in a cool, dark, dry place celeriac will keep for a couple of weeks. Once cut sprinkle with lemon juice as the flesh browns easily. Simmer for 10-15 minutes. Celeriac is delicious raw, combined with carrot and mustard in a salad, or cooked, coated with a Stilton sauce.

CHAYOTE, CHOW CHOW, VEGETABLE PEAR, CHRISTOPHENE or CHOKO

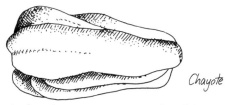

Chayote

Different countries have alternative names for this vegetable – in Britain it is known as "chow chow" or "vegetable pear", "christophene" in the West Indies and "choko" in Australia. Originally from Central America chayotes are grown in tropical and sub-tropical climates – in particular the Caribbean and South America. Brazil is the main exporter. In appearance they resemble a pale green, ribbed pear which feels hard even when ripe. Chayotes grow on a vine and are of the gourd family and have a delicate flavour – somewhere between that of courgettes, cucumbers and marrows. Nutritionally they are a fairly good source of vitamin C and also contain carotene and calcium. Chayotes are available all year round, choose small ones if possible, as these have a better flavour, and check that they are not bruised. Chayotes will keep well for 1-2 weeks in a cool, dark place. They must be cooked before eating – peel, halve, remove soft, flat seed and scoop out any fibrous strands. Dice and boil, or steam and serve in a cheese sauce. Alternatively do not skin but boil and then bake chayote halves stuffed with a tuna, tomato and pepper mixture. Since the flesh takes up the flavour of the cooking liquor chayotes can be used for sweet as well as savoury dishes.

CHICORY

Originally grown in Europe and Western Asia the plant's root was, and to a lesser extent, still is widely used as a coffee substitute. Belgium is now the main producer and exporter of chicory with supplies also coming from Holland and France as well as home grown produce being available. The spear-shaped heads are white with yellow tips. Obtainable throughout the year, choose those which are plump and have closely packed heads. Store in a dark place since chicory is very sensitive to light which causes increased bitterness, seen in greening of the leaf tips. Chicory will keep for 4-5 days in the salad drawer of the fridge. When preparing trim the root end and, using a small, sharp vegetable knife, remove the bitter core from the centre. The leaves may then be separated and used whole or shredded in salads, or the head braised with meat. Chicory is often accompanied with fruit to counteract some of its bitterness – in particular cranberries or oranges. Since this vegetable discolours on contact with air it is best to prepare chicory just before serving and sprinkle with lemon juice.

CHILLI

Of South American origin chillies are the fiery members of the capsicum family. Imports come from Cyprus, Kenya, India, Thailand, Israel, France and the Canary Islands. Produce is also now being grown in this country. There are two main varieties available – long, finger-length, thin, tapering pods, which are the hottest, or the plumper, shorter kind which are slightly milder. Colour is also an indication of strength – as green chillies ripen to red so their flavour intensifies. Although rich in vitamin C such a small quantity is added to dishes that their nutritional value is insignificant. Fresh chillies are available throughout the year although dried/powdered chilli may be easier to find and more convenient to use. Choose shiny, unwrinkled pods which are firm. Keep for up to a week in a cool place. Careful preparation is needed since the seeds irritate the skin so try not to touch them if possible, and wash hands immediately after handling. The seeds may be used in cooking, but are even hotter than the flesh, so are usually omitted. Chillies are added to meat, poultry and vegetable dishes to "spice-up" the flavour and are particularly popular in Indian cooking. An excellent burger relish can be made from onion, chillies and tomatoes, puréed together.

CHINESE CABBAGE or CHINESE LEAVES

This vegetable was eaten in Eastern Asia as long ago as the fifth century, although it was only introduced into Europe during the last century. Imports come from Holland, Spain and Israel and some is home grown. The leaves are pale green with long, fleshy white stalks, the heads resembling densely packed cos lettuces. Differing varieties produce heads of varying shapes, distinctively longer or more oval with crinkled or smoother leaves. As with other green leafy vegetables, Chinese leaves contain vitamin C, carotene, calcium, iron and protein. Available throughout the year this vegetable is particularly good value during the winter when other salad ingredients are expensive. Use as lettuce or cabbage (remembering that the leaves have a milder flavour than ordinary cabbage). Chinese leaves have the advantage of keeping well – store in the salad container of the fridge for 1½-2 weeks. Shred and boil or eat raw. Alternatively use leaves as a wrapping and fill with fish or meat to make savoury parcels.

COLOCASIA FAMILY

This group of rhizomes includes "dasheen"/"taro" and "eddoe". The starchy tubers are widely used in tropical countries in the same manner as potatoes are in the United Kingdom.

Dasheen/Taro – This irregularly shaped vegetable has a large main tuber which tapers off at one end, and can measure up to 12" (30cm) in length, with brown, hairy, scaly skin with pronounced rings. The white or yellow coloured flesh absorbs the flavours of other ingredients and as a result it is often paired with salt fish in Caribbean cookery as well as being added to soups and stews.

Eddoe – Eddoes were grown in Egypt and India long ago and are now also found in the South Pacific, West Africa, America, China and the West Indies, from where most imports come. The vegetable is relatively small, consisting of a central brown-grey bulb with numerous tubers sprouting from it. The inedible skin is tough and hairy and envelops the milky white flesh which is slightly sticky. Choose firm, blemish-free samples and cook in the same way as potatoes.

DUDI, DOODI or DOODHI

Imported from Kenya and Cyprus dudi have only recently become available. Round or long varieties exist – the former measuring about 4" (10cm) across whilst the latter resembles a baseball bat and may measure between 7" – 24" (18cm–60cm) in length. Dudi have smooth, fairly thin, pale green skins with seeded flesh. They may either be peeled before steaming, boiling or frying, or halved and baked with a stuffing. Since the flesh has no distinct flavour it soaks up those of the ingredients with which it is combined. Halve, scoop out seeds and fill with cooked minced beef spiced with curry paste, mango chutney and a little chopped tomato. Bake at 200°C, 400°F, gas 6 for 45-50 minutes.

ENDIVE

The value of this vegetable was exploited long ago by Greeks and Egyptians before it was subsequently brought to England by the Romans. Some endive is home grown with other produce imported from Europe. Broadly speaking there are two varieties: winter, or "curly" endive, which is available from September to November, and Batavian endive, or escarole, whose leaves are broader and less curly and is in season from September to April. Both have a bitter taste. Endive have green leaves surrounding a yellow heart, which has been blanched by tying the central leaves together before the plant is fully grown. When buying look for firm, fleshy, white stalks and fresh looking leaves. Endive does not keep very well, so store refrigerated for 1-2 days only. Wash thoroughly and add to salads or cook in a similar way to cabbage. Endive contributes vitamin C, carotene, calcium, potassium and iron to the diet.

FENNEL

Also alluded to as "finocchio" or "Florence fennel" to avoid confusion with the herb, the Italians have a passion for this aniseed flavoured vegetable. Indeed Italy, Spain and Holland are the main exporters with a little being grown in the United Kingdom and France. Similar in colour and ribbing to celery fennel has a bulbous, fleshy base with protruding stalks and green, feathery leaves which add flavour to stock as well as making an attractive garnish. Available at all times during the year buy weighty bulbs with tightly packed, "meaty" leaves. Avoid any with blemishes or which are dark green. To prepare; trim base and

84

stems, either thinly slice and toss raw into salads, halve and poach for 15-20 minutes, or steam as an accompaniment to fish, poultry or veal. Store fennel in the salad drawer of a fridge for 2-3 days.

Fennel

GINGER ROOT

Indian in origin ginger is still very much an integral part of Indian and Oriental cuisine. Imports come from the West Indies, South America, Brazil, Australia, Fiji and Kenya – countries where the rainfall is high and the soil fertile. Ginger is the rhizome of a tropical plant, beige-grey in colour, a swollen looking, knobbly root. Since it is basically a flavouring only relatively small quantities are used, hence its nutritional value is insignificant. Available throughout the year buy small pieces at a time and keep any remaining ginger wrapped and in a cool, dark, place for 2-3 weeks. To prepare; peel away thin skin to reveal fibrous, yellow, juicy flesh. Either chop finely or grate, and add to salad dressings, stir-fry dishes, stews, chutneys or sweet dishes such as puddings, cakes and biscuits.

GOURDS

This family is comprised of summer and winter varieties. The former have thin, tender skins and seeds which are eaten as well as the flesh, whereas winter squash have to be peeled, and the seeds removed. These also require longer cooking.

Spaghetti squash – a winter variety, these are large, heavy gourds with smooth, yellow skins, somewhat resembling honeydew melons. Their white, spaghetti-like flesh accounts for their other name of "vegetable spaghetti". The squash is boiled whole, the flesh being then scooped out and flavoured with cheese or tomato.

Butternuts – a half way house since they may be pickled in the summer, in which case they are tender, or in the autumn when they are usually parboiled, baked and stuffed or used in pickles. Butternuts originally came from tropical America and are now grown in North America and Europe. Similar in shape to a large, yellow, smooth-skinned avocado pear they can be purchased whole or halved.

Custard marrows – a summer squash, also sold as "golden patty pans" – which are smaller, about the size of a large tomato. In appearance custard marrows resemble a fluted yellow or white lantern. To prepare; trim away green stalk and steam whole, or halved, for 25-30 minutes. Patty pans have a slightly bitter flavour. Sauté with bacon and onion for about 10 minutes, add chopped parsley and season to taste. Place in a serving dish, scatter breadcrumbs and cheese over mixture and grill until crisp and golden. Other members of the gourd family which are becoming increasingly available are: chayotes, dudis, karellas, tindoris and pumpkins.

KARELLA

Originally from Kenya these gourds, similar in appearance to a small, thin, knobbly cucumber, have a bitter flavour. This can be reduced by soaking slices of the vegetable in water, or sprinkling with salt for 1-2 hours prior to cooking. Karella are a good source of iron, carotene and vitamin C and also contain a useful amount of fibre. Choose firm, bright green specimens, avoiding any which show signs of yellowing. Karella are very popular amongst the Asian community used as a side vegetable, in pickles and curries. To prepare; thickly peel ridged skin. The seeds may either be eaten or discarded.

LETTUCE

Iceberg – an American bred variety of lettuce also popular in Europe, iceberg derives its name from its original method of storage – under layers of crushed ice. Imports come from America and Spain. A tightly packed, round, cabbage-sized, heavy head with leaves curling at the ends, iceberg lettuces are pale green in colour, crisp and keep better than any other variety. Usually purchased wrapped in cling film, simply peel off as many leaves as are required at one time and keep remainder in the fridge for up to 2 weeks. Iceberg's are at their best during the winter months, do not need washing and have very little waste. Usually eaten raw in wedges or shredded, the lettuce cups may be filled with a fruit and nut salad.

Lamb's – also know as "corn salad", "mâche" or "lamb's tongues" because of the size and shape of the leaves, lamb's lettuce is produced commercially in Italy, Holland and France, although most is locally grown. Not strictly of the lettuce family it is a good source of carotene and vitamin C. Due to its expense it is not widely available, although restaurants often include the leaves as part of a mixed salad. The heads are loosely packed, and the soft green leaves have a delicate, slightly bitter flavour which is said to be at its best when lambing begins. Although it is available all year, peak supplies are to be found from October to April. Keep refrigerated for a couple of days at the most, and wash well before serving raw as an accompaniment to cold meats, or with chopped hard boiled egg and soured cream dressing.

MANGE-TOUT, SNOW or SUGAR PEA

In addition to home grown supplies imports come from Guatemala, Spain, France and Kenya. The whole pod is eaten, "mange-tout" being French for "eat all". Look for flat, pale green pods with small protrusions indicating the tiny, undeveloped peas. These are sweet because of their relatively high proportion of sugar which converts to starch as the pea matures. Nutritionally they are higher in protein than most vegetables, contain a considerable amount of fibre and a valuable quantity of iron and carotene. Mange-tout are available during spring and early summer. Keep for 1-2 days in the salad compartment of the fridge. To prepare; top and tail, removing the stringy spine, and wash. Mange-tout are best served steamed or lightly boiled for about 5 minutes, so that they keep their crispness and colour. The pods are particularly suited to stir-fry dishes – combine with fish, mushrooms and sweetcorn.

MOOLI, MOULI, RETTICH or ICICLE RADISH

Imported from Holland, Kenya and Italy mooli are similar in shape to a swollen, cylindrical carrot, but twice as long with a smooth, thin, white skin. In flavour they are milder than the common red salad radish and more bitter. Available all year round look for firm, clean roots. Peel, slice or grate, and eat raw or cooked, tossed in vinaigrette or as a side vegetable. Mooli contain less calcium and iron then red radishes but almost twice as much vitamin C.

OYSTER MUSHROOMS

A recent variety to appear on the supermarket shelves and very popular in France, most are imported from Holland although cultivation methods are being experimented with in this country. Called oyster because of their slight resemblance in flavour and the shape of their caps, to the seafood, these mushrooms are fan-shaped with fully exposed grey-fawn gills. Slightly tough and meaty in texture they must be cooked before eating. Wild the mushrooms grow on trees, and under cultivation on straw. Store refrigerated for 4-5 days. Look for mottle-free velvety caps when buying and fresh looking gills. To prepare; remove short stem and rinse. Oyster mushrooms take 5-8 minutes to cook and retain most of their water content. Excellent in casseroles they add a novel touch to dishes, having a stronger flavour than ordinary mushrooms.

OKRA, LADIES FINGERS, BHINDI, GUMBO or BAMIA

Okra

Also known as "ladies fingers" in Britain, "bhindi" (Asia), "gumbo" (America) – where it plays a major role in Creole cookery and is the basic ingredient of the dish named after it, and "bamia" (Middle East). Used for thousands of years, okra was originally grown in Africa from where it subsequently spread to America. Imports come from Kenya, Cyprus and the Caribbean. The long five-six sided dark green pods taper at one end, thus resembling "fingers" and vary between 2"-5" (5cm-12.5cm) in length. Usually slightly furry, the whole of the pod is eaten and has a delicate flavour. Inside are a mass of tiny seeds and on cooking the mucilaginous juices form a viscous paste, thus having thickening properties for sauces and casseroles. Okra contributes fibre, calcium, carotene, vitamin C, niacin and some protein to the diet. Available all year, most plentiful supplies are found from summer through to autumn. Look for firm, crisp pods which show no signs of browning. Buy slightly under-ripe for preference, since the pods become tough and flavourless as they age. Store for 2-3 days only. Careful preparation is necessary – if the pods are cut they lose their shape; thinly slice off the cap/stalk and simmer for 10-15 minutes. Alternatively, add to stews 15-20 minutes before the end of cooking. Okra combine well with tomato and chicken – as used in South American and Mediterranean cooking, and are also good served in curries or sweet and sour dishes.

PAK-CHOI or PAKSOI

Similar in flavour to Chinese leaves/spinach, pak-choi originated in South East Asia and is now imported from Holland. Resembling a loosely packed head of celery in shape the long, white stalks culminate in a head of rich green leaves. Both stalk and leaves are eaten – either boiled or sautéd for 4-5 minutes, or raw, chopped into salads. Availability fluctuates, but pak-choi are at their best towards the end of the year. Store in the salad drawer of a refrigerator.

PALM HEARTS

Grown in Brazil palm hearts are the tender young shoots of certain varieties of palm trees. The tough bark of the tropical plant is removed to reveal the pliable hearts. Available canned in brine they need no further cooking, just rinse and add to salads, or reheat and serve with a chicken liver and red wine sauce as a starter.

PLANTAIN

This vegetable is one of the staples of the African diet as well as being extensively used in West Indian and Central American cookery. Resembling a large banana in appearance their colour alters from green when unripe, through to yellow and finally black, their sweetness correspondingly increasing as they ripen. Nutritionally plantain are a good source of carotene, vitamin C, potassium and fibre. A dry, starchy vegetable, look for green-yellow produce and store for 2-3 days, depending on ripeness, at room temperature. Plantains must be cooked before eating. Normally they are baked or slit and boiled in their skins, which can then be easily peeled. Either serve sliced or mashed as an accompaniment to meat and fish, or try cooking with tomatoes, chillies and beans and serve with noodles.

SWEET POTATO

South American in origin the sweet potato is now grown in most tropical countries. It was the initial variety to be brought to England from the New World, however subsequently the potatoes we eat today were generally preferred and sweet potatoes are now regarded as unusual. Americans still prefer them though and export them along with Israel and the West Indies, thus facilitating a year round supply. Sweet potatoes are an irregular shaped, elongated tuber, tapering at one end and with a reddish-brown, slightly ridged skin. The colour of their flesh ranges from white through to a pinky-orange and exudes a slight stickiness. As their name suggests a sugaryness can be detected in their flavour. Sweet potatoes are an excellent source of carotene and contain valuable amounts of vitamin C, as well as some calcium and iron. In terms of carotene, vitamin C and fibre they are considerably richer than ordinary potatoes. When buying look for firm tubers, which are not shrivelled or blemished, and store for 1-2 weeks only. Peel in the same way as for potatoes and boil, fry or roast, or bake in skins. Sweet potatoes make an excellent accompaniment to bacon and ham, meat and poultry. Alternatively they can be used for a dessert – mashed and mixed with brown sugar, spices and butter and sprinkled with an oat and coconut crumble topping.

PUMPKIN

Much respected in the USA which boasts its pumpkin pie, pumpkins are also grown in Asia and Mexico. A member of the gourd family pumpkins vary in size, but tend to be relatively large, have an inedible orange skin, and yellow-orange flesh. Their flavour is delicate and slightly sweet – making them suitable for sweet and savoury dishes. Pumpkins are about 95% water and hence baking or steaming (for 20-30 minutes) are the most appropriate forms of cooking. Nutritionally they are a good source of carotene and calcium. In season from July to November pumpkins may be bought whole and kept for a fortnight, or in slices and eaten after a couple of days. Peel and remove seeds before cutting into chunks and steaming. Serve coated with a cheese sauce, stuffed or puréed. Pumpkins also make excellent soup. The seeds are a valuable food in their own right – rich in iron and the B vitamins. Composed of about 30% protein and 40% fat, when roasted they make a tasty nibble and may be sprinkled over other vegetables or added to salads to give a crunchy texture.

RADICCHIO

Related to chicory radicchio is sometimes sold as red chicory. A small, leafy vegetable with a bitter flavour imports come from Italy, where chicory first grew wild, and Holland. Found throughout Southern Europe, especially France, the crinkled burgundy leaves have broad white veins and are in season from September to May. A good source of vitamins, especially vitamin C, radicchio can be stored for up to 4 days in the salad drawer of a fridge. To prepare; slice off root, separate leaves and rinse. Radicchio are fairly expensive, therefore combine with other salad ingredients.

SALSIFY or VEGETABLE OYSTER

Also known as "vegetable oyster" because of the resemblance of flavour and texture, salsify is very much a European vegetable – having originated in France and Germany it was the Spanish who subsequently cultivated it. Although some home grown produce is available salsify comes in quantity from Belgium and France and is available from October to spring. In appearance it resembles a long, creamy coloured, thin parsnip. A fairly good source of calcium and iron, look for regular shaped tapering roots which are relatively clean. Handle carefully since they damage easily and store in a cool, dark place for 3-4 days. To prepare; scrub or peel thinly, cut into 1"-2" (2.5cm-5cm) pieces and drop into acidulated water to prevent browning. Salsify naturally exudes a sticky, milky substance when cut. Simmer for 10-15 minutes. This vegetable has a delicate flavour, with a hint of asparagus. Use raw in salads, sprinkled with lemon juice, or as a side vegetable. Combine with chicken or fish in bakes, gratins or pies.

SCORZONERA

This is black-skinned salsify which originated in Southern Europe. A small amount is grown in this country but imports from Belgium and Holland are relied upon. Scorzonera has purple-brown-black, earthy skin with protruding stubble. Available throughout winter and spring prepare and use as for salsify. Make a niçoise style salad with cooked salsify, tuna fish, green beans, red kidney beans and tomatoes and serve with a yoghurt and French dressing vinaigrette.

SEAWEED

One of the primary plants of this planet seaweed has yet to be nurtured or developed to any real extent by man. Relegated to use as a fertiliser, only in the Orient is it's potential realised. Over 2,500 varieties exist and since the characteristics of these vary according to geographical location and season, classification tends to be somewhat loose. Edible seaweed, sea vegetable or kelp as it may alternatively be called, can be roughly categorised as red or brown algae – although some green algae is also consumed. Dulse and carrageen (Irish Moss) fall into the first group whilst kelp, a larger variety, is an example of brown seaweed. This aqueous plant grows naturally on the rocks of sea beds. In Japan seaweed is farmed in unpolluted waters. Once cut it floats to the surface where it is hauled in in nets and despatched to be cleaned, dried and packed as quickly as possible to avoid nutrient loss. Sealed packets of dried seaweed have an indefinite shelf life, and even once opened may be kept in an airtight container for 4-5 months. Imported varieties are marketed under such names as "kombu" – available in sheets, strands, strips or powder, this can be eaten raw in salads or added to soups and casseroles as a thickener. "hiziki" – long, black, spaghetti-like strands, "nori" – sold in sheet form and "wakame" which must have its central core removed. Dulse is a broad leafed variety favoured in Ireland, as is Irish moss which is matted in appearance. Laver grows off the coast of the British Isles and is still popular in Wales where it is sold chopped and cooked as laverbread. Nori is the nearest Japanese equivalent. Most seaweeds require soaking for 10-15 minutes before cooking to ensure thorough removal of sand particles and to soften the vegetable. Primarily a seasoning seaweed can be added to soups and stews, or used as a thickener or gelling agent in desserts and savoury jellies. It may also be used as a vegetable or added to salads. Agar-agar is particularly popular amongst vegetarians as a substitute for gelatine, although it gives a cloudy result. First manufactured in China it is a blend of over 30 different types of seaweeds. Follow directions on packet ensuring that the powder/flakes have completely dissolved in boiling liquid, and use in sweet or savoury recipes. Carrageen is also used as a gelling agent, but does not form such a firm gel and requires straining. Both may prove to be useful alternatives to gelatine in setting fruits such as kiwi, which contain an enzyme known to break down the protein in gelatine. Nutritionally seaweed is rich in the B group vitamins and the minerals calcium, potassium and iron, and is the world's richest source of iodine, essential for the prevention of goitre. Seaweed also contains protein and some fat and is available in tablet form as a food supplement. This vegetable is credited with such attributes as protecting and cleansing the bloodstream, soothing stress and aiding respiratory problems. It is also a laxative.

SWEETCORN (whole baby cobs)

Sweetcorn, "maize" or "corn-on-the-cob" as it is often alluded to, has been grown since at least 1100 AD. Native to Central and South America, maize is the staple food in diets of much of Southern and Central America and Mexico. Baby sweetcorn are immature cobs harvested whilst still very young. They are sweeter than when allowed to ripen fully since not so much sugar has turned to starch. Baby sweetcorn are a good source of fibre as both core and kernels are eaten. They also contribute carotene, vitamin C, iron and other minerals to the diet. Fresh or pre-cooked canned baby corns are available. The former imported from Kenya and Thailand are found between December and April. Look for pale, undamaged cobs and store in a cool, dark place for 2-3 days. Baby sweetcorn are widely used whole, or sliced, in Oriental cuisine, adding a crunchy texture as well as colour to stir-fries and salads. Cook fresh cobs for 5-10 minutes.

SWISS CHARD or SEAKALE BEET

This vegetable is related to the beetroot family and grows well in temperate climates. Similar to spinach, but with fleshy white stalks, darker green leaves and a milder flavour, Swiss chard is a good source of vitamin C. Available in late spring through to the end of summer, choose fresh looking, shiny leaves and eat as soon as possible. Both the leaves and the stalks may be eaten – the stalks being served in a similar way to celery, whilst the leaves are "sweated" as a side vegetable or may be filled with a savoury stuffing.

TINDORIS

A mild gourd resembling tiny water melons in shape and colour, (although only 2" (5cm) long and ¾" (2cm) in diameter) tindoris turn orange and soft when over-ripe. Imported from Kenya during November – April, the skin is slightly tough, but usually eaten, and the flesh packed with edible seeds. Tindoris tend to be a little bitter and their flavour lies somewhere between courgettes and gherkins. On cooking they turn a paler green. Simmer whole for 15 minutes or slice and sauté for 5-10 minutes. They can also be eaten raw to give a crisp texture to salads and are traditionally served with curries as a side dish.

VINE LEAVES

The young leaves of the grape vine, originally from the Mediterranean, vines are still grown in this area as well as in the Middle East, with main imports coming from Greece and Turkey. The dark green leaves are vacuum packed in brine and must be soaked in boiling water for at least 20 minutes, rinsed under cold water and drained before they are ready for use. Only in the countries where they are grown are they available fresh. Renowned as the casing for dolmas, which are vine leaves stuffed with spiced rice and lamb, the leaves have a distinctive flavour, are relatively inexpensive and can be packed with a variety of fillings – experiment with chicken, raisins, tarragon and rice, or peanuts, bacon, mushrooms and breadcrumbs served with a tomato sauce.

Vine Leaves

WATER CHESTNUTS

The roots of an Oriental water plant used for centuries in Chinese cooking. Water chestnut bulbs are the size of a two pence coin and white in colour. They have a crisp texture and little flavour. A carbohydrate food imported into this country in cans, simply drain, slice and reheat in stir-fried dishes.

YAM

Less familiarly known as the "Indian Potato" (as a result of the escalation of West Indian immigrants who use yams as the equivalent of potatoes in this country), this vegetable is the tuber of a tropical vine which originated in China but is now grown widely in the West Indies and Pacific Islands. Imports come from the West Indies, Central America and Brazil. Yams may grow up to 1 foot (30cm) long, have a thick bark-like skin, which varies from fawn to pink in colour, and moist creamy flesh. Slightly higher in calories than potatoes, boiled yams contain about the same amount of protein and vitamin C, and slightly more fibre. They also keep well. Peel and cook in a similar way to potatoes – boil, bake, roast or fry. Yams discolour in the atmosphere so once prepared cover with water to which a little lemon juice has been added.

Globe Artichokes with Blue Cheese Sauce

The tangy Stilton sauce can be made while the artichokes are cooking. Use low fat cheeses if available and serve as a rich starter or a mid-day main course.

2 globe artichokes
lemon juice for sprinkling
3fl oz (75ml) dry white wine
½ small clove garlic, crushed
4oz (125g) Stilton cheese, grated
2oz (50g) Cheddar cheese, grated
2 teasps (2 × 5ml spoons) cornflour
2 teasps (2 × 5ml spoons) kirsch
1 teasp (5ml spoon) lemon juice
black pepper

1. Slice stalk from artichoke base and 1" (2.5cm) off the head. Trim remaining leaves with scissors so that tops are flat. Wash and sprinkle with lemon juice to prevent browning.

2. Place artichokes upright in a tightly fitting pan and pour in water to come half way up sides. Bring to the boil, cover and simmer for 25 minutes until a leaf can be pulled out easily. Drain and allow to cool slightly.

3. Pull back leaves to reveal hairy choke in the centre. Using a sharp teaspoon remove inedible fibres to expose greyish base.

4. Meanwhile place wine and garlic in a small pan. Bring to the boil, add cheeses and cook until just melted and smooth.

5. Blend cornflour with kirsch and lemon juice. Add to pan with pepper, bring sauce to the boil and simmer for 2-3 minutes until thickened.

6. Pour into artichoke shells and serve at once.

Serves 2.

Artichokes with Watercress

The contrasting flavours of watercress and artichoke make an unusual vegetable dish, a perfect accompaniment to meat dishes when entertaining. Use any milk not absorbed for soup or a sauce.

    1lb (450g) Jerusalem artichokes, scrubbed or peeled
    lemon juice
    1 bunch watercress, washed and roughly chopped
    1 onion, thinly sliced
    nutmeg
    salt and freshly ground black pepper
    ¼ pint (150ml) milk

1. Grease a 2 pint (1 litre) ovenproof dish. Slice artichokes thinly and place in a bowl with water and lemon juice to cover while preparing remaining ingredients.

2. Drain artichokes, arrange ⅓ over base of dish. Sprinkle with ½ the watercress and onion. Season. Repeat layers ending with artichoke.

3. Pour milk over vegetables, cover and bake at 180°C, 350°F, gas 4 for 1-1¼ hours until artichokes are tender.

Serves 4-6.

Brinjal Boats

Serve these tasty vegetarian boats with rice and baked tomatoes.

3 aubergines could be substituted for the brinjals which are not always available. If so, allow about 10 minutes longer cooking time.

6 × 4oz (125g) brinjals
2 teasps (2 × 5ml spoons) oil
1 medium onion, thinly sliced
1 clove garlic, crushed
1 medium green pepper stalk and seeds removed, thinly sliced
4oz (125g) mushrooms, washed, dried and sliced
7.51oz (213g) can red kidney beans, drained
4 tablesps (4 × 15ml spoons) water
2 tablesps (2 × 15ml spoons) tomato purée
½ teasp (2.5ml spoon) dried basil
salt and pepper

Topping
1oz (25g) wholemeal breadcrumbs
1oz (25g) Cheddar cheese, grated

1. Drop brinjals into boiling water and cook for 10-15 minutes until just soft. Drain and halve lengthways. Remove stalks if wished. Scoop out seedy flesh and chop. Drain shells.

2. Heat oil. Add onion, garlic and pepper and cook for 4-5 minutes. Stir in mushrooms and cook for a further 4-5 minutes.

3. Stir in remaining ingredients, including brinjal pulp, bring to the boil, cover and simmer for 15 minutes, removing lid for last 5 minutes of cooking. Adjust seasoning.

4. Divide filling between brinjal shells. Place on a greased baking sheet and sprinkle breadcrumbs and cheese over top. Bake at 200°C, 400°F, gas 6 for 15-20 minutes.

Serves 6.

Celeriac, Chicken and Bacon Pie

A warming, layered winter pie. Serve with gravy, crisp cabbage and carrots.

Pastry
12oz (350g) wholemeal flour

pinch of salt
6oz (175g) ½ vegetable fat, ½ polyunsaturated margarine
6 tablesps (6 × 15ml spoons) cold water

Filling
1¼lb (600g) celeriac
1 tablesp (15ml spoon) lemon juice
12oz (350g) chicken fillets
2oz (50g) polyunsaturated margarine
1 teasp (5ml spoon) vegetable oil
8oz (225g) back bacon, roughly chopped
4 tablesps (4 × 15ml spoons) finely chopped parsley
¼ pint (150ml) chicken stock
1 (size 4) egg, beaten

1. Rub fats into flour and salt until mixture resembles fine bread-crumbs. Add water and mix to a stiff dough. Wrap and chill while preparing filling.

2. Thickly peel celeriac. Grate and blanch in boiling water with lemon juice for 2 minutes. Drain well.

3. Slit chicken fillets almost in half, open out flat and place between two sheets of greaseproof paper. Hammer out with a rolling pin until thin. Dice into "bite sized" pieces.

4. Heat margarine and oil. Add chicken and fry for 1-2 minutes until sealed. Remove from pan with a slotted spoon. Add bacon and cook for 1-2 minutes. Drain well.

5. Roll out ⅔ pastry and use to line a 2 ¾ pint (1.65 litre) pie dish.

6. Place half the celeriac over pastry, scatter half the bacon on top and sprinkle with half the parsley. Make a layer with all the chicken, then repeat layers with parsley and bacon, finishing with celeriac. Pour in stock.

7. Brush pastry edges with beaten egg. Roll out remaining pastry and use for the pie top, re-rolling any leftovers to make rose leaf garnishes. Brush with egg, make a small slit in pastry to release steam and bake at 200°C, 400°F, gas 6 for 20 minutes. Reduce temperature to 180°C, 350°F, gas 4 and continue cooking for a further 25 minutes.

Serves 6.

Souffléd Smoked Ham and Cheese Chayote

Served with salad and a jacket potato stuffed chayote makes a satisfying main course.

   1 chayote
   2oz (50g) low fat Cheddar cheese, grated
   2oz (50g) smoked ham, finely chopped
   1oz (25g) wholemeal breadcrumbs
   1 tablesp (15ml spoon) chopped parsley
   ¼ teasp (1.25ml spoon) powdered mustard
   pepper
   1 (size 3) egg, separated

1. Scrub chayote and simmer whole for 30 minutes. Drain, halve and remove large flat seed. Scoop out flesh leaving a ¼" (6mm) thick shell. Turn shell upside down to drain, and chop flesh.

2. Combine cheese (reserving a little for sprinkling), ham, breadcrumbs, parsley, mustard, pepper and egg yolk with chayote flesh.

3. Stiffly whisk egg white and fold into stuffing mixture. Pile into shells. Sprinkle with reserved cheese and bake at 200°C, 400°F, gas 6 for 20-25 minutes until puffy and golden.

Serves 2.

Sweet-Sour Chicory and Liver

Put 6oz (175g) brown rice on to boil and by the time this dish is cooked the accompanying rice will be ready to serve.

   2 tablesps (2 × 15ml spoons) vegetable oil
   1 medium onion, thinly sliced
   1 medium green pepper, stalk and seeds removed, sliced
   4 tablesps (4 × 15ml spoons) seasoned flour
   1lb (450g) lambs' liver, sliced
   ½ pint (300ml) stock
   15oz (425g) can pineapple pieces in natural juice, drained
   3 heads chicory, quartered and washed
   2 tablesps (2 × 15ml spoons) sherry

1. Heat oil, add onion and pepper and fry for 10 minutes.

2. Coat liver in flour, add to pan with any remaining flour and cook for 2-3 minutes.

3. Blend in stock, bring to the boil, add pineapple, chicory and sherry. Cover and simmer for 15 minutes, stirring occasionally. Adjust seasoning if necessary and serve with rice.

Serves 6.

Eddoe and Tuna Patties

Substitute eddoes with potatoes or yam, depending on availability, and serve with tomato relish.

1lb (450g) eddoes, peeled
7oz (198g) can tuna in oil, drained and flaked
3 medium gherkins, finely chopped
2 tablesps (2 × 15ml spoons) finely chopped parsley
salt and pepper
1 (size 4) egg, beaten
2oz (50g) wholemeal breadcrumbs

1. Simmer eddoes for 15 minutes or until tender. Drain well and mash.

2. Add tuna, gherkin, parsley and seasoning to taste.

3. Divide mixture into 6 and form into patties, about 3″ (7.5cm) in diameter.

4. Dip each in egg then breadcrumbs and place on a greased baking tray. Bake at 200°C, 400°F, gas 6 for 15 minutes. Turn over and cook for a further 5-10 minutes until golden. Serve hot.

Makes 6.

Chinese Okra Omelettes

A complete main dish. Prepare all the raw ingredients in advance and cook just before you are ready to eat. Blanching heightens the okra's colour and softens the fibrous pod.

Filling
3oz (75g) okra, stalk removed, sliced into ½" (12.5mm) lengths
2 teasps (2 × 5ml spoons) vegetable oil
1 teasp (5ml spoon) finely chopped root ginger
1 teasp (5ml spoon) sesame seeds
½ small clove garlic, crushed
½ small red pepper, stalk and seeds removed, thinly sliced
1oz (25g) button mushrooms, washed, dried and thinly sliced
2oz (50g) shelled prawns
2oz (50g) beansprouts
2 small tomatoes, roughly chopped
salt and pepper

Omelettes
1 teasp (5ml spoon) vegetable oil
4 (size 3) eggs
2 teasps (2 × 5ml spoons) water
salt and pepper

1. Blanch okra in boiling water for 5 minutes. Drain.

2. Heat oil. Add ginger, sesame seeds and garlic. Fry for 2-3 minutes. Add okra, pepper and mushrooms. Cover pan and cook for 5 minutes. Stir in prawns, beansprouts and tomatoes. Season to taste and cook for a further 10 minutes.

3. While filling is cooking heat oil in a 7" (18cm) omelette pan. Pour off any excess. Lightly whisk together 2 eggs and 1 teasp (5ml spoon) water. Season and pour into pan. Fork set egg to the middle, tilting pan to allow uncooked egg to run to the edge. Cook for 1-2 minutes until golden underneath.

4. Slide omelette onto serving plate, divide filling, spoon half onto omelette and fold over. Use remaining ingredients to make second omelette. Serve at once.

Serves 2.

Plantain and Veal Wheels

A novelty dish for casual entertaining. Serve with a green leafy vegetable.

2 ripe plantain, approximate weight 1lb (450g)
3 tablesps (3 × 15ml spoons) oil
8oz (225g) veal mince
2oz (50g) button mushrooms, washed, dried and finely chopped
¼ teasp (1.25ml spoon) dried marjoram
salt and pepper

1.   Peel plantain and slice into four lengthways. Heat 2 tablesps (2 × 15ml spoons) oil in a large frying pan. Add plantain and fry for 3 minutes, until just brown. Drain well.

2.   Mix together veal, mushrooms and marjoram, season to taste. Form into eight balls.

3.   While the plantain are still warm, coil each around a veal ball and secure with cocktail sticks.

4.   Add remaining oil to pan and fry plantain wheels for 10 minutes until golden and the veal is cooked. Drain well, remove cocktail sticks and serve.

Serves 4.

Curried Lamb with Tindori

The crunchy tindori add a refreshing coolness to curry dishes.

2 tablesps (2 × 15ml spoons) oil
12oz (350g) lean lamb, diced
1 large onion, sliced
1 clove garlic, crushed
¼oz (8g) root ginger, finely chopped
2 teasps (2 × 5ml spoons) curry powder
1 teasp (5ml spoon) garam masala
½ pint (300ml) meat stock
juice of 1 lime

1 tablesp (15ml spoon) mango chutney
salt
12oz (350g) aubergine, wiped and sliced
8oz (225g) tindori, washed and dried

1. Brown lamb in 1 tablesp (15ml spoon) oil. Drain and set aside. Heat remaining oil, add onion, garlic, ginger, curry powder and garam masala and cook for 3-4 minutes.

2. Blend in stock, lime juice, chutney and season to taste. Return meat to pan and bring to the boil. Cover and simmer over a very low heat for 1 hour, stirring occasionally.

3. Add aubergine and tindori and cook for a further ½ hour. Serve on a bed of basmati rice.

Serves 4.

Chicken and Corn Vine Leaves with Lemon Sauce

These colourful parcels with their tangy sauce are very economical and at the same time unusual. Serve accompanied by jacket potatoes and baked tomatoes.

8oz (227g) packet vine leaves in brine

Filling
8oz (225g) chicken fillet
1 small onion
7oz (198g) can sweetcorn kernels, drained
4oz (125g) carrot, grated
2oz (50g) brown rice, washed
1oz (25g) sunflower seeds
finely grated rind of ½ lemon
½ teasp (2.5ml spoon) dried mixed herbs
salt and pepper

Sauce
½ pint (300ml) chicken stock
¼ pint (150ml) white wine
2 teasps (2 × 5ml spoons) cornflour
juice of ½ lemon

1. Pour boiling water over vine leaves and leave to stand for 20-30 minutes. Rinse with cold water and drain.

2. Mince chicken and onion. Mix with remaining filling ingredients.

3. Lay vine leaves, vein side uppermost, on work surface. Divide filling between each, placing slightly towards stalk end. Fold stalk end, then both sides of the leaf over filling and roll up to make a parcel. (Do not roll too tightly since the filling will expand slightly on cooking.)

4. Lay vine parcel flat over the base of a large, shallow pan. Pour over stock and wine, bring to the boil, cover and simmer for 1 hour.

5. For the sauce: drain off cooking liquor and measure ½ pint (300ml). Blend cornflour with lemon juice. Pour on reserved juices, bring to the boil and simmer for 1-2 minutes until thickened.

6. Allow 2-3 parcels per person and serve with sauce.

Makes about 20 parcels.

CHAPTER 6
Milk Products and Vegetable Oils

MILK PRODUCTS

Increased interest in lower fat foods has led to a surge in the development of modified forms of dairy produce. Some, such as low fat cream and low fat hard cheeses, involve modern processing techniques to achieve a product with similar characteristics to their traditional counterpart. Whilst other products have, by nature of their natural nutritional profile, found new popularity – such as buttermilk and smetana. Generally, the nutritional value of these foods will be similar to that of milk – rich in protein, calcium and vitamins A and D – only in a condensed form.

BUTTERMILK

Originally, as its name suggests, buttermilk was the liquid leftover as a result of butter making. Now it is manufactured from pasteurised skimmed milk, soured with a special culture to thicken it. Consequently it has a very low fat content. Similar in colour, texture, flavour and nutritional value to very low fat natural yoghurt buttermilk can be used in place of it in salad dressings, puddings or drinks – indeed buttermilk based fruit drinks are available. The milk is traditionally used in scone and soda bread making, its acidity combining with a bicarbonate raising agent to aerate the baked goods.

CHEESE

Numerous cheeses are appearing on the market with reduced fat contents, aimed at serving general demand rather than specifically for slimmers. In addition cheese suitable for vegans is also now available. The production of cheese involves a starter being added to the milk, which causes it to separate into curds and whey. Pressure is then exerted on the curds to expel the whey, leaving a firm cheese. Therefore

105

the harder the cheese, the longer its shelf life, the stronger its taste and the higher its nutritional value since it is concentrated. Cheeses are a good source of protein and calcium. Those with a high fat content will also contain more of the fat soluble vitamins A and D.

Low Fat Soft Cheeses – soft cheeses have a relatively high water content since the curds are not pressed. Made from cow's milk they have a lower percentage of fat, varying between 5%-10%, than full fat cream cheeses which are made from ripened cream and are about 45% fat. However, they can be used for the same purposes – cheesecake fillings, cake icings, dips, low fat spreads, stuffings for potatoes (delicious combined with chopped ham, sweetcorn and parsley), or puddings with added puréed fresh fruit and a little icing sugar or honey to sweeten. Even lower fat cheeses made from skimmed milk – such as Fromage Blanc and skimmed milk Quark are available, and these contain less than 1% fat. They have an acidic flavour and very soft consistency.

Half the Fat Hard Cheeses – presently Cheddar, Cheshire, Edam and blue cheese types are available. These have the same properties as the full fat versions – can be sliced or grated and cooked, although they tend to toughen more readily, so should be added towards the end of cooking – but are only about 15% fat. Their protein value remains the same.

Vegetarian Cheeses – up until now rennet, which is obtained from calves' stomachs, was the enzyme culture used to coagulate the milk proteins in cheese making. However, the manufacture of a vegetable rennet starter made from a microbial enzyme has meant that cheeses for vegan vegetarians are now available. Skimmed milk is combined with sunflower and soya oils to replace the traditional butter fat from cow's milk and has the added bonus of making the cheese higher in polyunsaturated fatty acids than ordinary cheese. Cheddar, Double Gloucester and Cheshire are the more common varieties available. Nutritionally there is very little difference between the fat and protein values, although reduced fat vegetarian Cheddar is also available.

CREAM SUBSTITUTES

An increasing range of non-dairy "creams" are appearing on the shelves. Produced from a blend of vegetable oils combined with buttermilk and butter, long life varieties are also available. These "creams" have the advantage of being cheaper, although nutritionally similar, than ordinary cream. In addition low fat varieties, which contain half as much fat as standard single (18% fat) or double (48% fat) cream are available. The "creams" can be used in place of their traditional dairy counterparts although they may take longer to whip and tend not to hold their shape quite so well.

GOAT'S MILK

Increasing in availability goat's milk is more easily digested than cow's. Slightly higher in calories (due to its fat content), it is lower in vitamins A and D but appreciably higher in iron and calcium. The protein values are comparable. In fresh or powdered form the milk is prized by those with an intolerance to cow's milk. Natural and flavoured yoghurts in addition to goat's cheese can now be readily found. The milk has a pleasant, but distinctive taste, and retails (as does soya milk) at about 1½ times the price of cow's milk.

SMETANA

Similar to yoghurt and buttermilk, but with a higher fat content, smetana is manufactured from skimmed milk and milk solids which have been innoculated with a lactic culture. The creamed variety has added cream and contains 12% fat, double the fat content of ordinary smetana. Smetana has a pleasant sharp taste, is fairly thick and can be used in both sweet and savoury dishes in place of soured cream. Add chopped spring onion, tuna and tomato relish to make a tasty jacket potato topping. When adding to casseroles or soups do so at the last minute since smetana separates on boiling. Delicious combined with fresh fruit purées it makes a refreshing end to a meal. Traditional Russian smetana has a much higher fat content and is equivalent to soured cream. Although smetana does not whip to hold its shape it retails at less than half the price of double and soured cream making a very attractive alternative.

GREEK YOGHURT

Yoghurt is an ancient product, references to it being found in the Bible. Its discovery was probably an accident – the combination of heat and aging producing a fermented product, and now it is widely used throughout the world, in particular in the Middle East and Asia. Yoghurt is produced from pasteurised homogenised milk which has been innoculated with bacterial cultures in order to ferment the sugar lactose to lactic acid which sours and thickens the milk. Made from whole, semi-skimmed or skimmed milk, yoghurt's nutritional value is similar to that of the milk from which it was made. Basically there are two types of Greek yoghurt, both made from whole milk – strained, which uses cow's milk, and sheep's milk yoghurt.

The strained yoghurt is thick and creamy, the straining process ensuring a concentrated source of milk. It is consequently higher in nutrients than yoghurt made from whole milk, containing about 10% fat as opposed to 4% in whole milk natural yoghurt. In terms of protein it contains 6%, whereas low fat natural yoghurt has just over 1%. Sheep's milk yoghurt contains 6% fat and is ideal for those allergic to cow's milk. It has the familiar acidity of yoghurt which the strained type lacks, and is also less rich. Alternatively sold as ewe's yoghurt it may be bought flavoured with fruit juices. Greek yoghurt is more stable in cooking than low fat yoghurts, and will not curdle if heated with cornflour or flour. The Greeks have used yoghurt for centuries in cooking and there are many superstitions concerning its link with living to a ripe old age. Traditionally it is served simply with honey. Incorporate yoghurt into salad dressings – flavoured with herbs, garlic and lemon juice, dips, curry sauces, ice creams and cold desserts. Thick Greek yoghurt makes an excellent substitute for cream, is more refreshing and lower in calories. Store yoghurt in the fridge for several days, making sure that it is consumed within the sell by date. It can be frozen for up to three months but is best sweetened first to avoid separation on defrosting.

Greek Yoghurt

OILS

Oils from many different sources are now becoming commonplace on supermarket shelves as interest in their use as opposed to animal fats increases. Fats and oils (which are liquid at room temperature) both contain saturated and polyunsaturated fatty acids, but in varying proportions. Animal fats are more likely to be high in saturated fat, whereas the majority of vegetable fats are high in polyunsaturates. The dietary interest in these fats has arisen from the evidence to suggest that polyunsaturated fatty acids lower the level of blood cholesterol – whilst saturated fats raise levels of cholesterol in the blood. Since high levels of blood cholesterol are thought to be one of the causes of coronary heart disease, we are being urged to increase the amount of polyunsaturated fats eaten at the expense of saturated fats.

Most oils are extracted from seeds or nuts, either by mechanical pressure or the use of solvents. Cold pressed oils tend to be the most expensive since, to prevent damage to nutrients (particularly the fat soluble vitamins A, D, E and K), colour, and flavour of the oil the seeds/nuts are crushed by a press and do not undergo any refining. This is not a very efficient method of extraction in terms of yield produced and prices are consequently high. The majority of oils are manufactured by dissolving the crushed seed/nut in a solvent, thus extracting the oil and leaving a solid residue. The oil is then heated to evaporate the solvent and purified to extend the shelf life by replacing antioxidants, which were destroyed in the heating process, lighten the colour and improve the taste and smell of the oil. The result of this process is economical for the manufacturer, since it is the most efficient means of extracting as much oil as possible, but does tend to result in a fairly bland oil. This has advantages for frying – since the oil is only there as a cooking medium, not a flavouring, but for salad dressings an oil with some taste is usually preferred. Walnut oil is a good choice but expensive.

Hydrogenation, that is the hardening of oils, has resulted in a wider application of vegetable oils for culinary purposes since as a fat they can be used as a substitute for animal fats for spreading and creaming.

A substantial proportion of oils available on the market are a blend from different sources. Cotton seed, coconut and palm oils are not usually sold on their own, but under the label "vegetable oil". By mixing different oils an improved product is obtained producing a good value cooking oil.

GROUNDNUT (PEANUT) OIL

See also "Nuts and Seeds" chapter.

Peanut oil is the third largest oilseed crop. The oil contains just over 30% polyunsaturated fatty acids, which is lower than most vegetable oils. Domestic uses include salad and cooking oil. On a commercial scale the residue meal which remains after the oil has been extracted is used for cattle food and fertiliser.

MAIZE (CORN) OIL

See also "Cereals and Grasses" and "Vegetables" chapter.

Pressed from the golden ears of corn which are used as a vegetable in this country maize has a very low oil content – about 2%. It grows well in warm climates with half of the world's total crop coming from America. The oil is high in polyunsaturated fatty acids – about 60%, and is used as a salad or cooking oil, as well as for baking.

OLIVE OIL

Extracted from the green or black fruit of the olive trees which yield 75-82% oil. The trees flourish on infertile, dry soil around the Mediterranean coastline – Spain, Italy, Greece and North Africa. The oil from the first crushing is the finest. Golden in colour it needs no refining. Pressure and heat are subsequently applied to extract as much oil as possible from the remaining mass. Olive oil is generally considered to be the finest available and prized for use as a salad dressing. It has a low smoking point and is therefore unsuitable for deep frying.

RAPESEED OIL

The only oilseed crop which is grown in Britain, the yellow flowers of rapeseed can be seen carpeting the countryside during spring until the end of July when they are harvested. Rapeseed has been grown in this country for centuries but it was not until recently that production has been stepped up to make it the third largest arable crop in the country. Other producers include France, Poland, China, India and Canada. Each pod bears about 14 very small, black seeds composed of about 40% oil. Rapeseed is a relatively inexpensive oil which is used for salad dressings and cooking.

SAFFLOWER OIL

Cultivated in Egypt, India, China and Southern Europe since ancient times safflowers are now grown mainly in Mexico (Mexican Saffron is another name for this plant – the petals being used as a substitute for saffron), America and Australia. Belonging to the thistle family the annual plants bear bright orange flowers in the summer. Safflower oil is richer in polyunsaturates than any other oil, being comprised of nearly 80%. Use as a salad oil or for frying.

SESAME OIL
See also "Nuts and Seeds" chapter.

Sesame seeds are composed of approximately 50% oil. The white seeds yielding a better quality oil than the black. Used for centuries in African and Far Eastern cooking sesame oil has the rare advantage of naturally containing the substance sesamol which prevents it from turning rancid – a particular bonus in tropical climates. Sesame oil is used in cooking, especially Chinese stir-fries, and as a salad oil.

SOYA OIL
See also "Pulses" chapter.

Soya oil is the major vegetable oil, accounting for about a quarter of all vegetable oil supplies. It is produced by crushing the soya beans which are then refined to obtain oil for use in cooking and salads. Soya bean oil has a high proportion of polyunsaturated fatty acids, about 60%. Commercially it is widely used in the manufacture of margarine.

SUNFLOWER OIL
See also "Nuts and Seeds" chapter.

Sunflower oil is particularly high in polyunsaturates containing roughly 70%. Use for salad dressings or as a cooking oil.

VEGETABLE SUET

Manufactured from vegetable oil rather than animal fat this suet can be incorporated into sweet and savoury dishes, in particular steamed puddings, pastries and stuffings. Based on palm nut oil, which unfortunately does not have a very high percentage of polyunsaturated fatty acids, this suet does provide a useful ingredient in vegetarian cookery. Properties are the same as for traditional suet as are storage conditions: once opened keep refrigerated.

Spicy Tuna Dip

Greek yoghurt gives this dip a rich, creamy flavour. Serve with a selection of crisp, fresh vegetables. Alternatively use as a topping for jacket potatoes.

7oz (198g) can tuna in brine, drained and flaked
4oz (125g) Greek strained yoghurt
1 hard boiled egg, shelled and chopped
1oz (25g) red pepper stalk and seeds removed, finely chopped
3 gherkins, finely chopped
1 tablesp (15ml spoon) mango chutney
1 teasp (5ml spoon) tomato purée
1 teasp (5ml spoon) Worcestershire sauce
½ teasp (2.5ml spoon) white wine vinegar
freshly ground black pepper
finely chopped parsley to garnish

Thoroughly mix all ingredients together. Serve dip in a bowl surrounded with vegetables – carrot, celery, cauliflower and pepper go particularly well – and garnished with parsley.

Makes ½ pint (300ml)

Cheese and Spinach Oat Turnovers

Oatmeal lends a "melt-in-the-mouth" crumbliness to this pastry. Ideal for packed lunches, picnics, or served hot with root vegetables.

Pastry
4oz (125g) wholemeal flour
2oz (50g) medium oatmeal
1 teasp (5ml spoon) dry mustard
¼ teasp (1.25ml spoon) paprika
3oz (75g) fat, ½ polyunsaturated margarine, ½ white vegetable fat
3 tablesps (3 × 15ml spoons) cold water

Filling

½oz (15g) polyunsaturated margarine
1 medium onion, chopped
small clove garlic, crushed
2oz (50g) button mushrooms, washed, dried and thinly sliced
4oz (125g) cooked spinach, chopped
1 tablesp (15ml spoon) sunflower seeds
grated nutmeg
2oz (50g) vegetarian Cheddar, grated

Topping

milk
vegetarian Cheddar, grated
paprika

1. Rub fats into flour, oatmeal and seasonings until mixture resembles fine breadcrumbs. Add water and mix to a stiff dough. Wrap and chill while preparing filling.

2. Melt margarine. Add onion and garlic and fry until lightly browned. Stir in mushrooms and cook for a further 2-3 minutes. Add spinach, sunflower seeds and season to taste with nutmeg. Leave to cool.

3. Roll out pastry into a 10" × 10" (25cm × 25cm) square. Cut into 4 × 5" (12.5cm) squares. Divide filling between squares and top with cheese. Brush edges with milk and fold pastry over filling to form a triangle. Seal edges and make a couple of slits in the top.

4. Place on a greased baking tray, brush with milk and sprinkle with cheese and paprika. Bake at 200°C, 400°F, gas 6 for 20 minutes until golden. Serve hot or cold.

Makes 4.

Calypso Cheesecake

This coral tinted cheesecake combines the subtle flavours of papaya and lime with a distinctive ginger base.

Base
1½oz (40g) polyunsaturated margarine
4oz (125g) ginger biscuits, crushed

Topping
8¾oz (250g) carton Quark low fat (4%) soft cheese
1oz (25g) caster sugar
finely grated rind and juice of 1 lime
0.4oz (11g) sachet powdered gelatine
1 papaya
5fl oz (142ml) carton ½ fat double cream, whipped

1. Melt margarine. Stir in crushed biscuits and press evenly over base of a 7″ (18cm) loose bottomed round cake tin. Chill.

2. Beat cheese, sugar and ½ lime rind until smooth. Sprinkle gelatine onto lime juice and dissolve over pan of simmering water. Leave to cool slightly.

3. Peel papaya, remove pips, reserve a few slices for decoration and purée remaining flesh. Stir into cheese mixture. Beat in gelatine. Fold in cream and pour over base. Level surface and refrigerate until set. Before serving decorate with papaya slices and reserved lime zest.

Serves 8

Passion Peach Mousse

Light and exotic, smetana adds tang to this fruity dessert.

14½oz (411g) can peach halves in fruit juice, drained and juice reserved
2 passion fruit
1½oz (40g) icing sugar
1 teasp (5ml spoon) lemon juice
0.4oz (11g) sachet powdered gelatine
½ pint (300ml) creamed smetana
2 (size 3) egg whites

1. Purée half the peaches. Halve passion fruit, scoop out seedy flesh and mix with peach purée, icing sugar and lemon juice.

2. Dissolve gelatine in 2 tablesps (2 × 15ml spoons) fruit juice. Allow to cool slightly. Whisk into fruit purée and stir in almost all the smetana.

3. Stiffly whisk whites and fold in. Pour into a 2 pint (1.2 litre) serving dish. Swirl in remaining smetana and chill until set. Decorate with slices of reserved peach before serving.

Serves 6-8

Fig and Pineapple Pudding

A tasty steamed pudding made with vegetable suet as opposed to beef- so vegetarians can enjoy it too!

Pudding
15oz (425g) can pineapple rings in natural juice
3oz (75g) self-raising wholemeal flour
3oz (75g) fresh wholemeal breadcrumbs
3oz (75g) vegetable suet
4oz (125g) dried figs, chopped
finely grated rind and juice of 1 orange
1oz (25g) soft brown sugar
½ teasp (2.5ml spoon) mixed spice
1 (size 3) egg, beaten
2 tablesps (2 × 15ml spoons) milk

Sauce
1 tablesp (15ml spoon) rum
1 teasp (5ml spoon) clear honey

1. Half fill a large pan with water. Place a trivet in the base and put on to boil.

2. Chop 2 pineapple rings and combine with flour, breadcrumbs, suet, figs, orange rind, sugar and spice in a bowl.

3. Add orange juice, egg and milk to give a dropping consistency. Beat well.

4. Grease a 1½ pint (900ml) pudding basin. Spoon in mixture and level surface. Cover with greased greaseproof paper or foil and secure with an elastic band. Place on trivet and boil for 1½-2 hours.

115

5. To make sauce: purée remaining pineapple with its juice in a blender/processor. Place in a small pan with rum and honey, heat through and serve with fig pudding.

Serves 6-8.

Caribbean Scones

These light, tangy scones are accompanied with a special date spread which is also delicious on bread, or as a cake filling.

8oz (225g) plain brown flour
1 teasp (5ml spoon) bicarbonate of soda
1 teasp (5ml spoon) cream of tartar
2oz (50g) polyunsaturated margarine
1oz (25g) desiccated coconut
1 tablesp (15ml spoon) soft brown sugar
finely grated rind of 1 orange
¼ pint (150ml) buttermilk
2 tablesps (2 × 15ml spoons) milk

Date Spread
4oz (125g) stoned dried dates, chopped
juice of 1 orange

1. Rub fat into flour and raising agents until mixture resembles fine breadcrumbs. Stir in coconut, sugar and orange rind. Add buttermilk and milk and mix to a soft dough.

2. Turn out onto a lightly floured surface and knead gently until smooth. Roll out to ¾" (2cm) thick and using a 2½" (6.5cm) fluted cutter press out 9 rounds, re-rolling as necessary.

3. Place on a greased baking sheet and bake at 220°C, 425°F, gas 7 for 10 minutes until risen and golden. Cool on a wire rack.

4. Place dates and orange juice in a small pan and simmer for 3-4 minutes until pulpy. Serve scones halved, spread with date mixture.

Makes 9.

CHAPTER 7

Sweeteners, Spreads and Preserves

In reply to the professional consensus to reduce the amount of sugar which we eat, several products, either with reduced sugar measures or which are naturally sweetened – such as preserves – are now becoming widely available. Sugar already present in the food is preferable to added refined sugar since, as well as being a concentrated supply of energy, it is usually found in conjunction with other nutrients – such as vitamins, minerals and trace elements – notably in molasses and unrefined brown sugars. Refined white sugar on the other hand is a form of pure calories, valuable only as a source of energy. Sugars also play a vital part in cooking – sweetening baked cakes, biscuits and puddings and bringing out the flavour of particular ingredients – such as tomatoes. Canned baked beans in tomato sauce are now available with no added sugar, but even these use apple juice as a natural sweetener to enhance the tomato flavour.

SWEETENERS

BROWN SUGARS

Sugar can be derived from cane, beet or tree sap. Sugar beet produces an identical white sugar to cane, but natural brown sugar cannot be derived from it since the bitterness of the beet's molasses makes for an unacceptable flavour. Maple syrup is the most common form of sugar from tree saps. It was not until the sixteenth century that regular, cheap supplies of cane sugar could be imported from the West Indies. First cultivated in India over 2,500 years ago sugar cane in now widely grown in tropical climates and in South America. Guyana, Barbados and Mauritius are among the main producers. The sugar cane plant resembles a bamboo, 1"-2" (2.5cm-5cm) in diameter, which grows to a height of 20 feet (6 metres). Lengths of cane for chewing on can now be bought from large supermarkets. Simply peel back the bark to reveal the white core and suck the sweet flesh.

Many different grades of brown sugar can be produced from sugar cane according to the stage of refining. Generally, the darker the resulting sugar the higher its molasses content and the stronger its flavour. However, brown sugar may also be manufactured from refined white sugar which has added caramel, refined molasses or sugar syrup, to give the desired flavour and colour to imitate raw cane sugar. To produce natural brown sugar the cane flesh is crushed and fed through rollers to squeeze out the juice, which is then refined to extract any impurities. The resulting juice is boiled to drive off the moisture and the saturated solution subsequently crystallised. At the first stage Demerara and a brown granulated sugar are produced – the latter is then washed to remove the molasses coating which causes the crystals to stick together, and thus ensures a free flowing sugar. Further crystallisation yields light brown sugar, dark brown sugar and molasses sugar – the crystals becoming progressively darker with a finer, stickier texture. Each type of sugar tastes different and is suited to particular culinary uses:

Brown granulated sugar – made from a very clear cane juice it is excellent for adding to beverages and in baking where white flour is used, giving a light coloured result.

Demerara sugar – originally produced in the Demerara area of Guyana, the large sized crystals give a crunchy texture to crumbles, breadcrumb toppings and biscuits.

Dark brown sugar – also sold as Muscovado or Barbados. This has a sticky texture and butterscotch-like flavour due to its molasses content.

Light brown sugar – also sold as light Muscovado. This is a beige coloured, soft sugar with a mild flavour. Suitable for cakes, biscuits and meringues it tends to be used in baking where a light result is desired. Dark brown sugar is particularly suitable for adding richness to dark cakes, such as gingerbread and rich fruit cakes.

Molasses sugar – also sold as black Barbados. This is almost black with a strong treacle flavour which makes it suitable for use in moist, dark cakes, Christmas pudding and also for savoury dishes – barbecue flavoured casseroles and sweet and sour recipes. This sugar is richer than the others in minerals and trace elements – both of which decrease as the sugar becomes lighter. In particular molasses sugar is a good source of iron and calcium. Dark brown sugar also contains valuable amounts.

118

MOLASSES

Similar in consistency and appearance to treacle, molasses is the residue syrup of sugar cane refining, a process in which as much sugar as possible is reclaimed from the sap solution. Molasses contains about 55% sugars compared with the 60-70% present in treacle, which is manufactured from a blend of molasses with added syrup to improve its otherwise rather bitter flavour. Blackstrap is the darkest form of molasses available and richest in minerals and trace elements – it is a particularly good source of iron and calcium, and also the vitamin B6 which is necessary for efficient assimilation of iron by the body. Molasses is hygroscopic and thus keeps breads and cakes made with it moist. As well as being used in baking it is also excellent for meat dishes – in bean and pork stew or as a glaze for joints.

MAPLE SYRUP

The maple tree, native to South America, is now cultivated in many parts of America and Canada. American settlers were taught by the Indians how to tap the maple trees during spring to obtain the sweet sap. Clear and flavourless when drawn from the sugar maple or black maple tree, the sap undergoes boiling to reduce it to a light caramel coloured syrup with its characteristic flavour. This syrup is fairly expensive and artificially flavoured syrups can now be produced at less cost. Therefore price is a good guide to authenticity Widely used in America for pouring over pancakes, waffles and ices, golden syrup is the nearest equivalent to maple syrup which we have in this country.

MALT EXTRACT

Produced from germinated grains (usually barley) which have been fermented, and are then concentrated into a syrup. Malt extract is made up of about 50% sugar, having a sweetness equivalent to molasses. Malt is added to many commercially prepared beverage powders – both for hot and cold drinks, and is used in breads (such as malt loaf) and cakes – to which it imparts a favourable moistness.

SPREADS

SAVOURY SPREADS

Sesame spread (tahini) and sunflower spread – see also "Nuts and Seeds" chapter.

These spreads are ideal for sandwiches, pitta fillings – with shredded lettuce and red kidney beans – and make a good base for dips and pasta sauces. The spreads have a slightly "gritty" texture and are high in fat – due to the nutritional value of the seeds – and because in their manufacture they are combined with oil.

FRUIT SPREADS

Sweeter than the no added sugar jams because a higher percentage of fruit pulp/concentrated juices are used, fruit spreads are made in the same way, using lime, apple or pear juices as their natural gelling agent. Consequently their calorific value is higher – more akin to that of ordinary jams. Flavours such as strawberry, apricot, black cherry, apple, plum or peach spread are available. These fruit spreads are excellent for those with a sweet tooth who prefer to eat sugar in its natural state.

PRESERVES

NO ADDED SUGAR PRESERVES

No added sugar jams are made from crushed fresh fruit boiled with concentrated apple juice (for increased sweetness and its valuable pectin content) with added lime juice to help set the jam. Since no sugar is added the calorific value of these jams is appreciably lower than that of traditional jams – in fact about half. A wide range of flavours are available – including strawberry, raspberry, blackberry, apricot and blackcurrant. Orange marmalade produced by the same method can also be readily found. These jams are sold as a completely natural product – free from any additives. Their one draw back is that once opened they must be kept refrigerated and consumed within three weeks. Use as a reduced calorie substitute for ordinary jam, or as an alternative to fruit purée – combined with natural low fat yoghurt for a tangy dessert, as a cheesecake topping or a fruit sauce diluted with fruit juice – try warming blackcurrant jam with orange juice to make a delicious sauce for pouring over steamed puddings or ice cream. No added sugar preserves may also be enjoyed by diabetics since the sugar is in a natural state and will therefore be broken down more slowly than refined sugar, enabling the body's system to cope with its digestion and assimilation.

REDUCED SUGAR PRESERVES

These have the advantage over ordinary preserves of containing a higher percentage of fruit (about 20%) which accounts for 40-50% of the jam's composition, and just over 30% of marmalade's, whilst having only half as much sugar. Since they are competitively priced with traditional preserves and have a similar shelf life (the no added sugar preserves are more expensive and must be eaten within 21 days) they can easily be incorporated into the diet providing a convenient way of reducing the family's sugar intake. The jams are available in all the basic flavours, as well as in some unusual combinations – such as kiwi and peach, and mixed berry. Slightly cloudy in appearance they have a tangy, fruity taste.

Tagliatelle and Mushroom Salad

This salad is best made a day in advance to allow the mushrooms time to absorb the various flavourings. Serve as a side salad or topped with Parmesan cheese for a main course dish.

    4oz (125g) tagliatelle verdi
    4oz (125g) Greek strained yoghurt
    4 tablesps (4 × 15ml spoons) milk
    2 tablesps (2 × 15ml spoons) red wine
    2 tablesps (2 × 15ml spoons) sesame spread
    2 tablesps (2 × 15ml spoons) chopped parsley
    1 teasp (5ml spoon) lemon juice
    Freshly ground black pepper
    7oz (198g) can sweetcorn kernels, drained
    6oz (175g) button mushrooms, washed, dried and quartered

1. Cook tagliatelle in plenty of boiling salted water, to which a drop of oil has been added, for 8-10 minutes until just cooked. Run under hot water and drain well.

2. Mix yoghurt with milk, wine, sesame spread, parsley, lemon juice and pepper.

3. Stir in sweetcorn, mushrooms and tagliatelle. Cover and leave for at least 4 hours.

Serves 6.

Malted Walnut Bars

These moist, nutty bars keep very well and are quick and easy to make. Use walnut oil if you have any.

    8oz (225g) self-raising wholemeal flour
    3oz (75g) soft brown sugar
    3oz (75g) walnuts, roughly chopped
    2 (size 3) eggs made up to ½ pint (300ml) with milk
    2fl oz (50ml) corn oil
    3 tablesps (3 × 15ml spoons) malt extract
    1 tablesp (15ml spoon) treacle
    1 teasp (5ml spoon) vanilla essence

1. Place flour, sugar and walnuts in a bowl and mix well.

2. Beat in egg mixture, oil, malt, treacle and essence to give a smooth batter. Pour into a greased and base lined 8" (20cm) square tin.

3. Bake at 180°C, 350°F, gas 4 for 25-30 minutes until golden. Turn out onto a wire rack. Cool. Cut into bars.

Makes 14.

Trinity Trifle

Apricot spread could equally well be used here. Allow to chill for a couple of hours prior to serving to ensure that the flavours have a chance to blend.

4 trifle sponges, broken
4 tablesps (4 × 15ml spoons) orange juice
3 tablesps (3 × 15ml spoons) sweet sherry
2 medium bananas, sliced
½ pint (300ml) natural low fat **set** yoghurt
6 tablesps (6 × 15ml spoons) peach spread
½oz (15g) desiccated coconut, toasted

1. Cover base of a 2 pint (1.2 litre) glass bowl with sponge pieces. Combine orange juice and sherry and sprinkle evenly onto crumbs.

2. Scatter banana slices over base.

3. Beat yoghurt until smooth. Mix in peach spread and spoon over fruit. Level surface.

4. Decorate with coconut and chill before serving.

Serves 6.

Dark Spice Cake

The inclusion of molasses and raw cane sugar in this cake imparts a rich colour and flavour and results in a moist texture. Wrapped in foil the cake actually improves with keeping.

4oz (125g) polyunsaturated margarine
4oz (125g) blackstrap molasses
2oz (50g) golden syrup
¼ pint (150ml) skimmed milk
8oz (225g) wholemeal flour
1 teasp (5ml spoon) bicarbonate of soda
1 tablesp (15ml spoon) mixed spice
1 teasp (5ml spoon) cinnamon
1 teasp (5ml spoon) allspice
4oz (125g) dark brown sugar
2 (size 3) eggs, beaten

1. Warm margarine, molasses and syrup in a pan until fat has melted. Do not allow to boil. Remove from heat, blend in milk and leave until cold.

2. Combine flour, raising agent and spices in a large mixing bowl. Rub in sugar. Make a well in the centre.

3. Stir eggs into melted mixture. Then pour into well and gradually draw in dry ingredients to make a smooth batter.

4. Pour into a greased and base lined 8″ (20cm) round cake tin. Bake at 150°C, 300°F, gas 2 for 1¼ hours, or until an inserted skewer comes out cleanly. Allow to rest in tin for 10 minutes before turning out onto a wire rack to cool.

Serves 16.

Hedgerow Crescent

Best served warm, brown flour gives a lighter result than wholemeal. Use a dark berry jam to show up swirls.

Batter

2 teasps (2 × 5ml spoons) dried yeast and 1 teasp (5ml spoon) sugar, or ½oz (15g) fresh yeast
3fl oz (75ml) hand hot milk
2oz (50g) strong brown flour

Dough

6oz (175g) strong brown flour
1½ teasps (1.5 × 5ml spoons) cinnamon
½ teasp (2.5ml spoon) salt
1oz (25g) polyunsaturated margarine
1oz (25g) caster sugar
1 (size 3) egg, beaten

To finish

4 tablesps (4 × 15ml spoons) no added sugar berry jam
beaten egg
flaked almonds

1. Sprinkle dried yeast and sugar over milk and leave for 5 minutes. Alternatively dissolve fresh yeast in milk. Stir in flour and allow to stand for 20 minutes until batter is frothy.

2. Rub fat into flour, cinnamon and salt. Add sugar. Stir egg into yeast mixture. Add to dry ingredients and form into a soft dough. Knead for about 10 minutes until smooth. Place in a greased polythene bag and leave in a warm place until doubled in size.

3. Roll out dough on floured surface into a 15″ × 9″ (38cm × 23cm) rectangle. Spread evenly with jam leaving a ½″ (12.5mm) border around edges. Roll up tightly from long edge. Place on a greased baking tray and form into a crescent. Brush with egg glaze. Slash dough at 1½″ (3cm) intervals, so that jam shows through. Sprinkle with flaked almonds, cover and leave in a warm place for about ½ hour until doubled in size.

4. Bake at 200°C, 400°F, gas 6 for 20-25 minutes until golden brown. Cool on a wire rack.

Serves 8-10.

Strawberry Caramel Pavlova

Brown granulated sugar flavours this marshmallow-like shell with a hint of caramel.

Pavlova
4 (size 3) egg whites
8oz (225g) brown granulated sugar
1 teasp (5ml spoon) vanilla essence
1 teasp (5ml spoon) cornflour
1 teasp (5ml spoon) malt vinegar

Topping
8oz (225g) strawberries
1 tablesp (15ml spoon) Cointreau
1 tablesp (15ml spoon) icing sugar
225g carton Greek strained yoghurt
¼ pint (150ml) whipping cream

1. Whisk egg whites until stiff. Gradually beat in sugar and continue whisking until the mixture forms stiff peaks. Fold in vanilla essence, cornflour and vinegar.

2. Mark an 8″ (20cm) circle on a piece of non-stick or greaseproof paper. Place on a baking sheet. Smooth meringue mixture over circle making a rim at the edge so as to form a "nest".

3. Bake at 140°C, 275°F, gas 1 for 1 hour. Switch off oven, leave door ajar and allow pavlova to crispen in oven overnight.

4. Reserve one strawberry for decoration. Hull and quarter remainder. Sprinkle with Cointreau and icing sugar and allow to stand until the fruit juices start to run. About 20 minutes.

5. Drain strawberries and reserve juices. Prick pavlova with a fork and spoon juices over.

6. Whip yoghurt and cream together until thick. Fold in strawberries and pile into meringue shell. Decorate with reserved strawberry and chill for ½ hour before serving.

Serves 8-10

CHAPTER 8
———Beverages and Juices———

BEVERAGES

Apart from tea and coffee there are many other beverages which are sold either as stimulant free substitutes, or simply as a flavouring for milk drinks. Most are grain based and often already sweetened. In addition herbal teas are enjoying popularity once again as an increasing number of people turn towards alternative forms of medicine to cure their ailments.

DECAFFEINATED COFFEE

Although weight for weight coffee contains less caffeine than tea, because more coffee is used to make a cup, coffee is the major source of caffeine. As a stimulant caffeine affects the central nervous system which can result in sleeplessness and lead to dependence. Consequently since the beginning of this century methods of extracting this alkaloid, whilst still ensuring that the coffee maintained its desirable flavour and aroma, have been sought. Early practices favoured the use of chemical solvents of which methylene chloride and ethyl acetate are still used today. Pioneered in the early 1900's the basic decaffeination process, followed even now, was developed in Germany. Green coffee beans are steamed to hasten solubility (warmth and moisture creating favourable conditions) and treated with a solvent (in which caffeine is readily dissolved) which is then drained off allowing the decaffeinated beans to be dried before they are roasted in order to bring out the characteristic taste and aroma of coffee. Nowadays the use of the natural solvents, water or carbon dioxide, to extract the caffeine are favoured. Both instant and filter decaffeinated coffee are available.

COFFEE SUBSTITUTES

Also referred to as "grain coffees", since they are based on roasted barley, wheat or rye, although chicory and dandelion roots (which belong to the same family) are also popular. The grains/roots are roasted

127

to bring out their full flavour before being ground and blended to give such combinations as; barley, rye and chicory, or wheat, bran and molasses. Hence a range of flavours to suit each individual's taste is available. These beverages have the advantage of not containing habit-forming caffeine. As for coffee boiling water is poured over the granules/powder, milk added if wished, and the drink sweetened to taste.

HERBAL TEAS

For centuries healing properties have been attributed to herbal teas. Also classified as tisanes, their therapeutic qualities are believed to relieve such disorders as asthma, arthritis, bronchitis, catarrh, fatigue, insomnia and even varicose veins. It would take a whole book to describe the varieties which can be found and their associated functions, however, some of the more widely available include; lemon balm, comfrey, fennel, dill, peppermint, elderflower and rose hip. Blends of herbal teas can also be found. The teas are simply the dried and crushed leaves of the plant and may be sold loose or as tea bags. Herbal teas are made in the same fashion as ordinary tea; infused for 5-10 minutes before being strained, and are usually served without added milk. Allow 1 teaspoon (5ml spoon) of tea per person, or if fresh herbs are used, 1 tablespoon (15ml spoon) of leaves which have been bruised in order to extract as much flavour as possible. Infusions of herbal teas can be used for cold punches, or in cakes and teabreads to give added moistness. These teas are low in tannin and, unlike ordinary tea which contains caffeine (although slightly less than is found in coffee), are caffeine free. In addition, a blend of Ceylon tea, the leaves of which have been specially treated so that the amount of caffeine present is negligible, are also available.

MALTED DRINKS

These came about as the result of work on diets for infants and invalids during the middle of the nineteenth century. Malt based drinks are easily digestible and contribute carbohydrate (mainly in the form of sugar, which accounts for 50-75% of the powder), fat (although at the most, this is about a third of the amount present in cocoa) and minerals to the diet, as well as the goodness of the added milk. Some are fortified with B vitamins and vitamin D. Different varieties of malted drinks are available, but basically they consist of a blend of barley and malt extract, powdered milk and sugar. Some are enriched with egg, and cocoa or carob may be added. Easy to prepare – just dissolve in hot or cold milk – they have a rich, creamy flavour. Malted milk drinks are sold primarily as soothing "nightcaps" but the powder/granules can also be used in baking – added to cakes, biscuits, puddings and sauces – in the same way as when using cocoa powder. Low fat versions are also available.

Herbal Teas,
Barleycup,
Malted drinks

JUICES

A variety of fruit and vegetable juices, apart from the standard orange, grapefruit, apple and tomato, are now enjoying increasing popularity. Home pressed juices are simple to make but time consuming and often work out to be more expensive than if bought. Water accounts for about 90% of fruit and vegetable juices, but despite this they are a valuable source of vitamins, minerals and enzymes making them an all round tonic for good health. They do not contain any fibre though since this is left behind when the liquid is extracted. However, some juices, such as apple, have a high pectin content which alleviates constipation, and orange and grapefruit juice are mild laxatives. Juices do not require digesting and are therefore quickly absorbed into the body, giving instant stimulation – hence their popularity served at breakfast – alerting the body for the day ahead. They also "wet" the appetite as a non-alcoholic aperitif before meals. It is the trace elements and enzymes present in the fruits/vegetables which are responsible for their vitality inducing properties; tomato juice contains manganese which helps settle stomach upsets, while the proteolytic enzymes in papaya (paw paw) juice are responsible for the digestion of protein. When making juices fresh fruits/vegetables should always be used since their nutrient value decreases on aging. Choose ripe, firm produce, scrub rather than peel, since many of the valuable nutrients lie just below the skin, and extract juice from raw fruits/vegetables with the aid of a mechanical press. These squeeze the juice from the pulp giving a clear liquid. A blender/processor is unsuitable since this simply makes a thick purée. As a warning, when preparing your own juices do not use any metal equipment, except for stainless steel, since metal reacts with the acids/alkalies in the fruits/vegetables causing discolouration. To benefit from their full goodness freshly pressed juices should be drunk at once.

FRUIT JUICES

The sales of fruit juices, fresh and long life, have soared over the last few years. The flavour and nutritional value of fresh juice is infinitely superior, however it does only keep for a week, whereas sterilised fruit juice has a shelf life of up to one year. Once opened both types should be kept under refrigeration and drunk within a week. Bottled and cartoned fruit juices are convenient for instant use although if freshly squeezed at home the juice will contain a higher proportion of vitamins since those which are heat sensitive will be destroyed during processing (vitamin C in particular). Oxidation (which occurs naturally in the atmosphere) also depletes vitamins, thus freshly pressed juices should be drunk immediately. The initial nutritional value of fruit juices is dependent on the variety of fruit used – most are valuable sources of carotene and vitamin C, with some of the B group present, and minerals – particularly iron in apricot, grape and strawberry juices. Fruit juices are preferable to squashes in terms of nutrients although, according to the degree of the squashes' dilution, their calorific values are similar. However, a comparison is difficult since the sweetness of the juices themselves differ – for example orange juice has half as many calories as pineapple. Fruit juices make refreshing appetisers mixed with lemonade or sparkling water, wine and a couple of ice cubes. In fact, served chilled, the clear juices – such as a grape, apple, pear and redcurrant, make a sophisticated substitute for wine. Non-alcoholic cocktails can be based on fruit juices blended with fresh fruit purée, lemonade and a flavouring – such as coconut cream. Care should be taken in giving too much citrus juice to children since the citric acid present in the juice interfers with the body's absorbtion of calcium and can cause tooth decay. It is therefore a good idea either to dilute the juice with water or ensure that citrus based fruit juices are served just before a meal. The wide range of flavours to choose from include such unusual types as apricot, passion fruit, pear, peach, plum, redcurrant, prune, blackberry and cherry. Combinations of juices – such as strawberry and apple may also be found, and juices made at home offer an even greater range. As a general guide 1lb (450g) apples will yield ⅓ pint (200ml) juice, whilst if a berry fruit is used ½ pint (300ml) is obtained.

Concentrated Fruit Juices – which have had most of their water content evaporated are also available, but in a more limited range. The evaporation process intensifies their sweetness making them an ideal base for fruit salads, drinks and sauces.

Fruit Syrups – which are thicker than juices (water accounts for only about a third of the syrup's weight, the rest is made up with sugar) are a blend of sugar, fruit pulp and water, boiled down to a pouring consistency. The addition of sugar takes the edge off the acidity of the fruit, but because it increases the calorific value concentrated juices are preferable. Syrups are delicious poured onto pancakes or ice cream, or blended with natural yoghurt and milk for a rich drink.

Fruit Drinks – are fruit juices with added water and sugar, their actual fruit content can be as low as 6%. Heat treated to prolong their shelf life, there are many unusual blends available which may be used in jellies and sorbets, but are usually just served chilled as a thirst quencher. Use as a base for punches – adding fresh strawberries and sliced cucumber in the summer or in winter months warming apple drink with a little cinnamon and a few cloves.

VEGETABLE JUICES

Carrot, tomato, mixed vegetable and beetroot are the main varieties of canned/bottled vegetable juices available. A wider range can be freshly pressed at home using leafy vegetables – such as cabbage, lettuce, spinach or watercress leaves, French beans, radishes, cucumber and celery, with the added nutritional advantages of a higher vitamin and mineral content. Drunk as an accompaniment to a meal, vegetable juices can also be used as a substitute for gravy, in refreshing savoury jellies for summer eating – set with agar agar or gelatine, or extended with fresh vegetables for a quick hot or cold soup.

Last Minute Soup

Made in seconds, carrot juice could equally well be used instead of tomato. Alternatively serve as a chilled aperitif.

Croutons
2 slices brown bread
2 teasps (2 × 5ml spoons) polyunsaturated margarine
½ small clove garlic, crushed

Soup
¾ pint (450ml) tomato juice
¼ pint (150ml) orange juice
¼ pint (150ml) low fat natural yoghurt
10 ice cubes
2 tablesps (2 × 15ml spoons) finely chopped parsley
1 teasp (5ml spoon) Worcestershire sauce
2 teasps (2 × 5ml spoons) soft brown sugar
black pepper
slice of orange and chopped parsley to garnish

1. Remove crusts from bread and slice into cubes. Melt margarine with garlic. Add bread cubes and turn until coated.

2. Spread cubes on a baking sheet and cook at 200°C, 400°F, gas 6 for 10 minutes, turning occasionally to ensure even browning. Cool.

3. Place remaining ingredients in a liquidiser/processor and blend until smooth.

4. Serve garnished with chopped parsley, a piece of orange slice and croutons.

Serves 6.

Fruity Yogshake

Greek yoghurt gives this drink an underlying rich creaminess. Drink straight away since otherwise the peach browns spoiling the delicate pink colour.

2 small peaches, stoned and roughly chopped
5oz (150g) Greek strained yoghurt
4 ice cubes
¼ pint (150ml) redcurrant nectar

1. Place chopped peach, yoghurt and ice cubes in a liquidiser/ processor and blend until smooth.

2. Gradually pour in redcurrant nectar.

3. Divide between two tall glasses and serve at once.

Serves 2.

Tropical Cream

A refreshing pudding for summer days.

0.4oz (11g) sachet powdered gelatine
1 pint (600ml) tropical fruit drink
5.29oz (150g) carton tropical fruit yoghurt
5fl oz (142ml) carton ½ fat double cream
2 tablesps (2 × 15ml spoons) icing sugar, sieved

1. Dissolve gelatine in 4 tablespoons (4 × 15ml spoons) of fruit drink. Allow to cool slightly and whisk into remaining liquid.

2. Pour a quarter of the jelly into a wetted 2¼ pint (1.3 litre) mould. Refrigerate until set.

3. Whisk together yoghurt, cream and icing sugar until mixture forms soft peaks. Fold into unset jelly and pour into mould. Refigerate until set.

4. Loosen around edges and turn out onto a plate just before serving.

Serves 6.

Coffee Orange Cake

A moist cake which could be served as a dessert gâteau. An alternative icing can be made by substituting the orange rind with 2 teasps (2 × 5ml spoons) decaffeinated coffee dissolved in ½ teaspoon (2.5ml spoon) boiling water.

¼ pint (150ml) milk
2 tablesps (2 × 15ml spoons) decaffeinated coffee
8oz (225g) self-raising brown flour
3oz (75g) soft brown sugar
3fl oz (75ml) corn oil
2 (size 3) eggs, beaten

Icing
5oz (150g) low fat soft cheese
1½ tablesps (1.5 × 15ml spoons) icing sugar, sifted
finely grated rind of 1 orange

1. Warm a little of the milk, add coffee and stir until dissolved. Blend into remaining milk.

2. Combine flour and sugar in a mixing bowl. Make a well in the centre and add coffee liquid, oil and beaten egg. Gradually draw in flour and mix to a smooth batter.

3. Divide mixture between 2 × 7" (18cm) greased and base lined sandwich tins. Bake at 190°C, 375°F, gas 5 for 15-20 minutes until risen and set. Cool on a wire rack.

4. Beat together icing ingredients. Use half to sandwich cakes together. Smooth remaining over top.

Serves 12.

Nutty Choco-Malt Snaps

These light, crisp biscuits have an intangible flavour and "moreish" nature.

4oz (125g) polyunsaturated margarine
3oz (75g) icing sugar, sifted
1 teasp (5ml spoon) vanilla essence
7oz (200g) self-raising brown flour
2oz (50g) malted chocolate drink
½ teasp (2.5ml spoon) bicarbonate of soda
2oz (50g) mixed chopped nuts
3 tablesps (3 × 15ml spoons) milk

1. Cream fat, sugar and essence until light and fluffy.

2. Combine flour, malted chocolate drink, raising agent and nuts. Fork into creamed mixture and add enough milk to make a soft dough.

3. Place level tablesps (15ml spoons), spaced well apart allowing room for the biscuits to spread, on greased baking sheets. Flatten slightly.

4. Bake at 180°C, 350°F, gas 4 for 12 minutes. Cool on a wire rack.

Makes 26-28.

Natures Store Tea Bread

Soaking the fruit in delicately flavoured rose hip tea ensures that the teabread keeps it's moistness for days after baking.

½ pint (300ml) strong rose hip tea
6oz (175g) stoned dried prunes, snipped
2oz (50g) sultanas
8oz (225g) self-raising wholemeal flour
1 teasp (5ml spoon) mixed spice
2oz (50g) polyunsaturated margarine
3oz (75g) soft brown sugar
1oz (25g) flaked almonds
1 (size 3) egg, beaten

To decorate
flaked almonds

1. Pour hot tea over prunes and sultanas and leave overnight to soak.

2. Rub fat into flour and spice. Stir in sugar and almonds. Add tea and fruit mixture and beaten egg. Mix well.

3. Spoon into a greased 2lb (900g) loaf tin, level surface, sprinkle with flaked almonds. Bake at 180°C, 350°F, gas 4 for 1¼ hours until an inserted skewer comes out clean. Turn out onto a wire rack and cool.

Serves 12.

Ruby Cup

A refreshing alternative to a wine-based punch. Allow drink to stand for 5-10 minutes to "mellow" before serving.

½ pint (300ml) red grape juice
4fl oz (125ml) port
soda water
4 slices of lemon
4 sprigs of mint
8-10 ice cubes

1. Combine grape juice with port. Make measure up to 1 pint (600ml) with soda water.

2. Add lemon slices, squeezing to extract some juice, with the mint and ice cubes.

Makes 1 pint (600ml)

Yoghurt Pear Sauce

A "zippy" sauce to spice up everyday sponge puddings, spoon over fresh pears or serve accompanied with shortbread.

½ pint (300ml) natural low fat yoghurt
4 tablesps (4 × 15ml spoons) pear juice concentrate
¼ teasp (1.25ml spoon) finely grated fresh ginger
good pinch of Chinese five spice powder

Combine all ingredients. Cover and chill before serving.

Makes approximately ¾ pint (450ml)

Blackcurrant Sherbert Sorbet

Quick and easy to make, using a fruit syrup saves having to extract juice from fruit and making a sugar syrup.

> ½ pint (300ml) blackcurrant syrup
> ½ pint (300ml) soda water
> 2 tablesps (2 × 15ml spoons) freshly squeezed lemon juice
> 2 (size 3) egg whites

1. Mix together blackcurrant syrup, soda water and lemon juice. Pour into a rigid container and freeze, uncovered, until half frozen.

2. Beat fruit mixture well to break up ice crystals. Stiffly whisk egg whites and fold in carefully.

3   Return to container, cover and freeze until firm.

Serves 8

Index

Notes

Notes

Notes

Notes